KT-431-850

access to sociology

CRIME, DEVIANCE *and* SOCIAL CONTROL

*Emma Wincup &
Janis Griffiths*

Series Editor: Paul Selfe

Hodder & Stoughton

A MEMBER OF THE HODDER HEADLINE GROUP

Orders: please contact Bookpoint Ltd, 39 Milton Park, Abingdon, Oxon OX14 4TD.
Telephone: (44) 01235 400454, Fax: (44) 01235 400454. Lines are open from 9.00–6.00,
Monday to Saturday, with a 24 hour message answering service.
Email address: orders@bookpoint.co.uk

A catalogue record for this title is available from The British Library

ISBN 0 340 749245

First published 1999
Impression number 10   9   8   7   6   5   4   3   2
Year   2005   2004   2003   2002   2001   2000

Copyright © 1999, Emma Wincup, Janis Griffiths

All rights reserved. No part of this publication may be reproduced or transmitted in any
form or by any means, electronic or mechanical, including photocopy, recording, or any
information storage and retrieval system, without permission in writing from the
publisher or under licence from the Copyright Licensing Agency Limited. Further
details of such licences (for reprographic reproduction) may be obtained from the
Copyright Licensing Agency Limited, of 90 Tottenham Court Road, London W1P 9HE.

Typeset by Transet Limited, Coventry, England.
Printed in Great Britain for Hodder & Stoughton Educational, a division of
Hodder Headline plc, 338 Euston Road, London NW1 3BH by Redwood Books,
Trowbridge, Wilts.

CONTENTS

ACKNOWLEDGEMENTS

We would like to thank Paul Selfe for inviting us to write this book, and for his helpful comments and advice. In addition, we are grateful for the extremely thorough and constructive guidance from Llinos Edwards in the organisation and production of this book.

SHREWSBURY COLLEGE LIBRARY

INV. No. L324991	DATE 5.11.01	
ORD. No. 10556	DATE 19.10.01	
ACC. No. 035793		
CLASS. No. 364 WIN		
PRICE £7.90	CHECKED T	

1

INTRODUCTION

HOW TO USE THE BOOK

EACH CHAPTER IN this book examines one or more of the central debates relating to the sociology of crime and deviance. The text is devised for readers with little or no background knowledge in the subject, and there are Study Points and Activities throughout to encourage a consideration of the issues raised. Student readers are advised to make use of these and answer them either on paper or in group discussion, a particularly fruitful way of learning; they will assist them to develop the skills of interpretation, analysis and evaluation. There are many ways of preparing for an exam, but a thorough understanding of the material is obviously crucial.

Each chapter is structured to give a clear understanding of the authors, concepts and issues that you need to know about. To assist understanding and facilitate later revision, it is often helpful to make concise notes.

MAKING NOTES FROM THE BOOK

Linear notes
- Bold headings establish key points: names, theories and concepts.
- Subheadings indicate details of relevant issues.
- A few numbered points list related arguments.

Diagram or pattern notes
- Use a large blank sheet of paper and write a key idea in the centre.
- Make links between this and related issues.
- Show also the connections between sub issues which share features in common.

Both systems have their advantages and disadvantages, and may take some time to perfect. Linear notes can be little more than a copy of what is already in the book and patterned notes can be confusing. But if you practise the skill, they can reduce material efficiently and concisely, becoming invaluable for revision. Diagrammatic notes may be very useful for those with a strong visual memory and provide a clear overview of a whole issue, showing patterns of interconnection. The introduction of helpful drawings or a touch of humour into the format is often a good way to facilitate the recall of names, research studies and complex concepts.

Activity

- Make a diagram to show the two ways of making notes with their possible advantages and disadvantages.

SKILLS ADVICE

Students must develop and display certain skills for their examination and recognise which ones are being tested in a question. The clues are frequently in key words in the opening part. The skill domains are:

1 **Knowledge and understanding:** the ability to discuss the views of the main theorists; their similarities and differences; the strengths and weaknesses of evidence. To gain marks students must display this when asked to *explain, examine, suggest a method, outline reasons*.
2 **Interpretation, application and analysis:** the use of evidence in a logical, relevant way, either to show how it supports arguments or refutes them. Students must show this ability when asked to *identify, use items A/B/C, draw conclusions from a table*.
3 **Evaluation:** the skill of assessing evidence in a balanced way so that logical conclusions follow. Students can recognise this skill when asked to *assess, critically examine, comment on levels of reliability, compare and contrast*, or if asked *to what extent*.

Activity

Draw an evaluation table, as below, using the whole of an A4 page. Examine studies as you proceed in your work and fill in the relevant details. Keep it for revision purposes.

Sociologist		
Title of the study	Strengths	Weaknesses
Verdict		
Judgement/justification		

REVISION ADVICE

- Keep clear notes at all times in a file or on disk (with back-up copy).
- Be familiar with exam papers and their demands.
- Become familiar with key authors, their theories, their research and sociological concepts.

Activity

Make and keep **Key Concept Cards**, as shown below.

COLLECTIVE CONSCIENCE

Key idea

A term used by **Durkheim** meaning:

- The existence of a social and moral order exterior to individuals and acting upon them as an independent force.
- The shared sentiments, beliefs and values of individuals which make up the **collective conscience.**
- In **traditional societies** it forms the basis of social order.
- As societies modernise, the collective conscience weakens: **mechanical solidarity** is replaced by **organic solidarity**.

Key theorist: Emile Durkheim

Syllabus area: Sociological Theories of Crime and Deviance: Functionalism

---

EXAMINATION ADVICE

To develop an effective method of writing, answers should be:

- **Sociological:** use the language and research findings of sociologists; do not use anecdotal opinion gathered from people not involved in sociology to support arguments.

- **Adequate in length:** enough is written to obtain the marks available.
- **Interconnected** with other parts of the syllabus (such as stratification, gender, ethnicity).
- **Logical:** the answer follows from the relevant evidence.
- **Balanced:** arguments and counter arguments are weighed; references are suitable.
- **Accurate:** reliable data is obtained from many sources.

The three skill areas on p 2 should be demonstrated, so that the question is answered effectively.

In displaying knowledge, the student is not necessarily also demonstrating interpretation:

- This must be specified with phrases like 'Therefore, this study leads to the view that…'.
- Sections of answers should hang together, one leading to the next. This shows how the question is being answered by a process of analysis based on the evidence.
- Reach a conclusion based on the evidence used and the interpretations made.

The skill of evaluation is often regarded (not necessarily accurately) as the most problematic. Evaluation means being judge and jury; the strengths and weaknesses of evidence are assessed and an overall judgement about their value is made. To evaluate an argument or theory, consider whether it usefully opens up debate and explains the events studied. Does it have major weaknesses?

Activity
Look through some past examination papers and pick out the evaluation questions. Underline the evaluation words and work out which skills are required.

COURSEWORK ADVICE

Coursework provides an opportunity to carry out a study using primary and/or secondary data to investigate an issue of sociological interest, and must address theoretical issues. The suggestions included at the end of each chapter may be adapted or used to generate further ideas. Final decision must be agreed with a teacher or tutor.

MAKING A PLAN

Before starting a piece of coursework, you should make a plan:

1 Read and make notes from articles describing research projects in journals.
2 Have a clear aim in mind; choose an issue that interests you and is within your ability.
3 Decide more precisely what you want to know; establish a simple hypothesis to test.
4 Select a range of possible methods; consider both quantitative and qualitative.
5 Decide on a range of possible sources of information.
6 List the people to whom you can seek help, perhaps including a statistician.

WRITING THE PROJECT

1 Seek frequent advice from a teacher or tutor.
2 Check the weighting for different objectives in the marking scheme.
3 Keep clear notes throughout, including new ideas and any problems that arise.
4 Limit its length (maximum 5,000 words).
5 Label and index the study in the following way:
   a **Rationale:** a reason for choosing the subject; preliminary observations on the chosen area
   b **Context:** an outline of the theoretical and empirical context of the study
   c **Methodology:** a statement of the methodology used and reasons for selecting it
   d **Content:** presentation of the evidence and/or argument including results
   e **Evaluation:** the outcomes are weighed and strengths and weaknesses noted
   f **Sources:** all the sources of information are listed.

OR

   a **Title**
   b **Contents**
   c **Abstract:** a brief summary of the aims, methods, findings and evaluation.
   d **Rationale**
   e **The Study**
   f **Research Diary**
   g **Bibliography**
   h **Appendix:** to include proposal for the study, single examples of a questionnaire or other data-gathering instrument and transcripts of interviews.
   i **Annex:** to include raw data gathered.

Paul Selfe
Series editor

2

DEFINING CRIME AND DEVIANCE

Introduction

CRIME AND DEVIANCE are among the obsessions of our society. We are fearful of crime and yet fascinated by it (Croall 1998). At the same time as we are horrified and frightened by crime stories, we are intrigued by crime and criminals. Films, newspapers and television programmes about crime form part of our staple media diet. However, these stories are often sensationalist and provide us with a particular view of crime. We hear most often about unusual or atypical crimes and this may distort our view of the problem of crime and may influence which types of crime we are afraid of.

In this chapter, we will look at a wide range of behaviours, some of which are criminal in our law and others which we may regard as deviant or socially unacceptable. Discussion will centre on various definitions of crime and deviance. A number of debates will be opened up for you to consider in more depth later in the text. When reading this chapter, or indeed the whole book, you should think about two key questions:

- What do you consider to be the strengths and weaknesses of the different definitions of crime and deviance put forward by sociologists?
- How might the reality of crime differ from images of crime presented by the media and politicians?

Table 1: *Theorists, concepts and issues in this chapter*		
THEORETICAL PERSPECTIVE	DEFINITION OF CRIME	VIEW OF CRIMINAL LAW
Functionalism	Crime is a violation of a legal code.	Criminal law reflects the norms of wider society.
Interactionism	Crime is a social construction.	Criminal law is created by members of society and is culturally and historically relative.
Marxism	Crime refers to acts of the powerless. The harmful acts of the powerful are not criminalised.	Criminal law reflects the interests of the ruling class.
Feminist and Critical Criminology	Crime is politically informed and linked to particular interests.	Criminal law reflects structured inequalities in society, eg class, ethnicity, gender.

Activity

Go through the television listing for any week with a highlighter pen; include Cable and Satellite channels. How many of the programmes are dramas or documentaries about crime or deviance? What proportion of the schedules do these programmes represent?

WHAT IS CRIME? WHAT IS DEVIANCE?

Crime is usually defined simply as a violation of the criminal law. Deviance is a much wider and vaguer concept than crime and is therefore more difficult to define. Deviance exists in relation to what is considered 'normal' in a society. Crime and deviance are overlapping in categories because criminal acts are often viewed as deviant acts. Most sociologists have focused their attention on criminal rather than other forms of deviant behaviour.

LEGAL CODES AND SOCIAL CODES

We can define crime as an act that breaks the criminal law and deviance as behaviour that breaks or departs from the norms of the majority in society. Using this definition, breaking a **legal code** makes someone criminal. Criminals are those who have broken the law and, if caught, the criminal justice system will apply legal sanctions against them.

Breaking a **social code** makes someone deviant. Sanctions will be applied to the deviant person, but these will tend to be informal and social. For example, an unwashed person in our society will be punished via social disapproval and unpopularity, but is breaking no laws and therefore no legal sanctions will be applied. Extreme deviant behaviour may result in a person being described as mentally ill. Deviance can be a far more difficult concept to handle than criminality because such moral decisions are often cultural and personal.

You should now understand that deviance and crime are different but linked ideas. Most criminal behaviour will involve breaking a social code as well as a legal code. However, this is not always the case. Criminal acts may not always be defined as an infringement of societal norms and values. This applies to serious offences, as well as the less serious ones. For instance, most people regard taking another person's life as a detestable offence. However, there are circumstances when behaviours, which the law would define as murder, could be regarded as socially acceptable, at least to some members of society. One example might be the doctor who gives a lethal injection to a patient who is terminally ill and wishes to die. This act is known as euthanasia or 'mercy killing' and there have been calls for this type of action to be decriminalised.

We are all capable of certain deviant acts. Most of us have committed criminal acts – few people can truly say that they never break any laws. There are circumstances when conformity is more deviant than rule-breaking. Anyone who has driven a car on a motorway will recognise that few cars travel within legal speed limits. Underage drinking can be regarded as a norm in our society as only a minority of people wait until their eighteenth birthday for their first taste of alcohol in a pub. These acts break a legal code but do not necessarily break a social code.

Activity
Consider the following crimes and ask yourself if you have ever done any of the following. Have you: 1   Kept money if you received too much in change? 2   Taken stationery or anything else from work or school? 3   Driven faster than the speed limit on a motorway? 4   Kept money that you found in the street? 5   Bought an alcoholic drink in a pub when you were under the legal age limit?

You may have been involved in these behaviours and may not even consider them socially unacceptable, but all are criminal offences. Often these behaviours are excused. They may be regarded by many people as events other than crimes.

For example, taking things from work may be viewed as a perk of the job. People are unlikely to be prosecuted for any of these acts because such behaviours are not only excused, they are usually undetected, ignored or not reported to criminal justice agencies.

Activity
If you found cash in the street, at what point would you feel it necessary to hand the cash in to the police? 5p? £5? £50? £500? Would you hand it in at all? Would it make a difference if it was in a wallet or purse? Do a survey of as many people as possible and consider the variations in the answers that you obtain.

There are a wide range of acts that are viewed by many as socially unacceptable, but which have yet to be criminalised. These acts might include creating environmental pollution or breaching health and safety legislation. If they are dealt with at all, these behaviours are seen as infringements of the *civil* rather than *criminal* law and thus attract relatively minor punishments. We can all think of behaviours which we think are socially unacceptable and which should be regarded as criminal. Equally, we are all likely to have different views about which acts these are, because the norms and values we adhere to are *cultural* and *personal*.

Our views on crime vary to a great extent. Societal reactions to various forms of crime are determined by more than the action itself, but sociologists disagree on what influences reactions to crime. In the most general of terms:

- Functionalists might argue that it is the impact on society that underlies the seriousness with which each crime is treated.
- Interactionists would be more concerned with the meanings attached to the particular acts by individuals and the application of the label 'criminal' or 'deviant' by society in general and the criminal justice system in particular.
- Marxists would suggest that the differences lie in the class, economic and power position of the person who has broken a law.

We explore these different theoretical perspectives throughout the text.

RETHINKING DEFINITIONS OF CRIME AND DEVIANCE

Crime and deviance may appear, at first glance, easy to define in terms of the infringement of legal codes and social codes. However, as the above discussion has shown, as sociologists it is necessary to adopt a more critical approach. Consider the following questions:

- Why are particular behaviours or acts deemed criminal whilst others are not?
- Are there behaviours that are inherently criminal?

- Who makes the law and whose interests does it serve?
- Do all members of society have the same norms and values?
- Whose norms and values are reflected in criminal law?

These questions have been the focus of considerable debate amongst sociologists working within different theoretical traditions and they provide the broad themes for this text.

Functionalists believe that there are shared norms and values within society on which criminal law is based. Their work is discussed in detail in Chapter 5. However, interactionist sociologists have suggested that crime is a social construction. They argue that society creates crimes because it makes the legal codes and breaking a legal code is regarded as criminal behaviour. Those who adopt this last approach point out that legal codes vary between different countries and between different historical periods in the same country. More importantly, they suggest that defining crime with reference to legal codes is limited. Instead, crime is seen as a consequence of societal interaction. Thus it is important to explore societal reactions to criminal acts.

A COMPARATIVE VIEW OF CRIME AND DEVIANCE

Legal and social codes differ between countries. These codes may be influenced by factors such as politics and religion. For example, the act of drinking alcohol in Britain is seen as acceptable, but in a country such as Saudi Arabia is an imprisonable offence. Equally, the possession and use of cannabis is illegal in Britain but in other countries, such as the Netherlands, it can be purchased legally.

CHANGING DEFINITIONS OF CRIME AND DEVIANCE

Definitions of crime and deviance vary over time. The concept of crime itself has not always existed and behaviours now considered criminal were previously defined as sinful, civil wrongs or private disputes (Sharpe 1996). There are many examples of acts which at particular points in time have been considered criminal and at other times have been seen as acceptable. To use the alcohol example again, in the US 1920s prohibition, legislation made the consumption of alcohol a criminal offence, but prior to this it had been seen as acceptable and legal behaviour.

Activity

1   Make a list of activities that are criminal in Britain but acceptable in other cultures.
2   Make a list of activities that were criminal in the past but are now perfectly legal.
3   Make a list of activities that would have been legal in the past but are now criminal.
4   What types of human activities are likely to be considered immoral and wrong in most cultures?
5   What types of human activities are most subject to cultural variation?

Crime and deviance can, therefore, be viewed as culturally and historically relative. Whether an act is judged criminal or deviant depends on the country in which it takes place and the point in time when it occurs.

Study point

The Popular Garden Annual (1929) advises that to obtain a graceful decorative border 'a few plants of the Hemp (Cannabis) might be included for the sake of the tall, leafy stems.' Consider how this quotation illustrates that crime and deviance can be said to be historically and culturally relative.

Interactionists focus our attention away from particular behaviours and instead consider societal and personal responses to crime and deviance. To illustrate, if a person steals something, a process of negotiation will take place between the rule-violator, the victim and the criminal justice system. The thief may be labelled as a criminal or charges may be dropped. Interactionists suggest that sociologists should not explore the act of theft because this behaviour in itself is not criminal. Interactionists argue we need to study the process of criminalisation: to examine the application of the rules in a society that forbids theft.

Consequently, they point out that the categories of crime and the criminal law are socially constructed products. There are no behaviours that are inherently criminal. Apply this logic to the act of killing somebody. In some instances, this act may be defined as murder, but in other circumstances it might be defined in other ways. For example, in war the act of killing could be seen as masculine, heroic or brave.

Interactionist definitions of crime and deviance add a new dimension to the debate but they leave a number of issues still to be explored:

● Who makes the law?
● Who enforces the law?

Those adopting a Marxist or critical criminological perspective have taken up these issues. These areas of debate will be opened up now but explored more fully later in this text (Chapters 5 and 6).

VISIBLE CRIME AND HIDDEN CRIME

Marxists suggest that acts are **made** criminal only when it is in the interests of the ruling class to define them as such. In capitalist societies, crime performs the vital function of diverting the attention of the lower classes away from the exploitation they face. It also allows the ruling class to establish political control over the lower classes.

Those working within the critical criminological tradition have taken up these views. **Box** (1983) suggests that the State is able to conceal and mystify the serious crimes of the powerful by focusing on crimes of the powerless. This tradition highlights the influence of class inequality but also inequalities linked to gender and ethnicity.

Murder! Rape! Robbery! Assault! Wounding! Theft! Burglary! Arson! Vandalism! These form the substance of the annual official statistics ... Aggregated, they constitute the major part of 'our' crime problem. Or at least, we are told so daily by politicians, police, judges and journalists who speak to us through the medium of newspapers and television. And most of us listen.

Box, 1983, p 1

For Box, the State cannot fully achieve this mystification without the help of the media who offer a particular, sensationalist and partial version of the crime problem. Hidden from view are crimes within the family, crimes of the market, crimes of the State and racial victimisation. We will explore these types of crimes in turn.

CRIMES WITHIN THE FAMILY

Popular images of the social world construct the home as a place of safety and public spaces as dangerous, particularly the streets of the city. However, feminist researchers have increasingly focused our attention on crimes committed within the home. Examples of such crimes include:

- domestic violence
- physical, sexual and emotional abuse of children
- elder abuse.

Whilst there is recognition that men may be the victims of domestic violence, victims of crimes within the family are usually women, children and the elderly.

Such crimes often remain hidden and there are numerous reasons why this is the case. **Saraga** (1996) offers a number of explanations:

- Victims may not tell anyone because they fear that no one will believe them.
- Victims may feel that speaking out will lead to more abuse.

- The offender is likely to be someone they are dependent on.
- The abuse takes place within an emotional relationship and the victim may love the offender.
- Victims may blame themselves or excuse the behaviour of the offender.

Studying family violence enables us to explore gender inequalities in society but also raises issues about what constitutes crime when it takes place 'behind closed doors'. For example, until 1990, the law did not recognise rape within marriage.

IN 1877, A MAN COULD BEAT HIS WIFE WITH A STICK - IF IT WAS NO THICKER THAN HIS THUMB

SO WHAT'S CHANGED?

WOMEN'S AID FEDERATION (ENGLAND) LTD
PO BOX 391, BRISTOL, BS99 7WS
TEL: 0272 428368 (helpline) 0272 420611 (admin)

CRIMES OF THE MARKET

Box (1983) suggests that most people accept the 'official view' of crime. Few are aware of corporate crimes conducted behind the closed doors of office suites or indeed how serious these crimes are. Crimes of the street remain at the centre of public attention and only occasionally does corporate crime receive media and criminal justice attention (Langan 1996).

The term 'white-collar crime' was first introduced by **Sutherland** (1949) and was used to refer to crimes carried out by those in the upper socio-economic classes. Researchers since then have broadened his definition to include offences committed by those in other social classes in the course of employment, or any abuse of occupational role.

Langan (1996) offers five categories of offence:

1   Large corporate crime committed by companies which might include offences against employees, the public or other firms.
2   Large-scale criminal corporations eg drug syndicates working on an international level.
3   Small-scale criminal firms eg garages selling fake MOT certificates.
4   Occupational crime committed by those taking advantage of their occupational position eg 'fiddling' expense claims.
5   Other white-collar crime eg tax evasion.

These behaviours are diverse, but there are some common features. They largely remain invisible and criminals are able to escape detection because crimes of the market are largely carried out by seemingly respectable people in the course of routine commercial activities. Such acts are unlikely to be detected or prosecuted and not all are defined as infringements of criminal law. However, such crimes affect all of us directly or indirectly (Croall 1993).

CRIMES OF THE STATE

The criminological gaze has rarely dwelt on those criminal actions perpetrated by the State itself (McLaughlin 1996a). Examples of such acts include massacres, tortures and illegal arms trading. These are arguably infringements of human rights. Such actions are rarely deemed criminal.

Activity
Research what you can about apartheid rule in South Africa, the rule of the generals in Argentina and Chile and the conditions experienced in Turkey and Iran by members of ethnic minorities such as the Kurds. You might get useful information if you write to Amnesty International.

Cohen (1993) argues that a culture of denial surrounds crimes of the State. He suggests that three statements are often given:

1   It doesn't happen here (complete denial).
2   If it does, 'it' is something else (eg self-defence).
3   Even if it is what you say it is, it is justified (eg protecting national security).

Some countries appear willing to move beyond the remit of national or international law to protect their own interests and seem able to commit terrible atrocities against their own minority groups and political opponents. In contrast, the same countries will use the criminal law to protect against threats to their own authority. They will imprison and execute 'criminals' guilty of opposing their mandate to rule.

RACIAL VICTIMISATION

Another invisible crime is the crime of racial victimisation. Racial victimisation in Britain has a long history. Concern about the phenomenon has only really been expressed in any significant way since the late 1970s. The extent of racial victimisation is not fully known since racially motivated crimes are rarely reported to the police. The British Crime Survey (Mirrlees-Black *et al* 1996) found that less than half of all racially motivated crimes were reported to the police. They estimate that 15 per cent of crimes committed against ethnic minorities are judged by their victims to be racially motivated.

In 1990s Britain, racial violence has received unprecedented attention. This is partly the consequence of the tragic case of Stephen Lawrence, a young black man who was murdered in London in April 1993. No-one has been charged with his murder. The case has led to a debate about the police response to racial violence and the role of the Crown Prosecution Service in taking actions against those believed to be responsible. This has resulted in inquiries into the criminal justice response and allegations of institutionalised racism within the police.

Moreover, racial victimisation became an issue debated in the 1997 General Election campaign.

> Britain is a multiracial and multicultural society. All its members must have the protection of the law. We will create a new offence of racial harassment and a new crime of racially motivated violence to protect ethnic minorities from intimidation.
>
> *Labour Party Manifesto, 1997*

Racially motivated offences have been included in the 1998 Crime and Disorder Act. Whilst the Government demonstrates a commitment to taking racial victimisation seriously, one question we must ask is whether it will actually lead to protection for ethnic minorities?

Again the issues that are raised by this discussion of racially motivated crime should direct you to consider the contested nature of the concept of crime. Another element which should become part of your thinking is the extent to which an action is defined as a crime via the workings of the criminal law and the criminal justice system.

Points of evaluation

The interpretation by sociologists of how crime is reported and perceived is influenced by the perspective they adopt in their analysis. Their various views may therefore be accepted by some and criticised by others:

1 Functionalists encourage the view that crime is a normal social event, but critics note that this justifies the imposition of severe rules and sanctions, especially on the powerless.
2 Interactionists have developed a refreshing look at the ways in which crime and deviance are defined by observers, but critics point out that this may lead to the view that no acts are in themselves deviant or criminal.
3 Marxists remind us of the significance of class factors, but some suggest that they neglect other important social divisions such as gender, ethnicity and age.
4 Feminists have usefully focused attention on the crimes affecting women. However, for some critics this is done too exclusively.

SUMMARY

Chapters 5 and 6 will revisit many of the theoretical perspectives introduced in this chapter and then explain to you the main ways in which sociologists have tried to explain criminal behaviour. The sociological perspectives discussed are each based on a particular view of crime and a particular view of criminal law. They vary significantly in the ways that they believe society is organised. You should refer back to Table 1 (page 7) when you read Chapters 5 and 6.

This introductory chapter has revealed some of the complexities that surround the study of crime and deviance. Sociologists adopt different theoretical perspectives, which in turn influence:

• the definitions that they use
• their view of social and legal codes
• the behaviours, which they see as making up the problem of crime.

The discussion in this chapter has probably raised more questions than it has answered. This was our intention. You need to develop a critical and evaluative approach to the subject matter which will allow you to score highly in examinations and coursework. You should bear in mind the issues raised in this chapter as you read the chapters that follow.

Key Concept Activity

Consider the following terms and look up the meanings in a variety of texts, CD-Rom encyclopaedias, or ordinary and sociological dictionaries. Note the differing definitions that are on offer:

- norms
- morals
- values
- crime
- deviance.

Do the definitions differ in detail? Can you come to an adequate working definition of the terms for yourself?

Group Work

1 As a group, choose 10 possible but real crimes, such as rape, bigamy, drug abuse, drunk driving and burglary. Each person should then question a wide variety of respondents noting age, gender and ethnicity. Ask which crimes they fear most, which are the worst for society and which should be punished most severely. They could rank the crimes in each of the categories offered. Pool your results. How unanimous are people in their perception of the severity of the crimes? To what extent does their fear of crime relate to the likelihood or possibility of being the victim?

2 Get into groups of three. One of you in each group is to be the law maker; he or she can speak and consult with the other two people. The other two people are only allowed to shake or nod their heads in response to questions. They must not speak, write or sign. The law maker has 10 minutes to devise a series of 10 rules, such as a code of conduct for people living in a house together.

At the end of the time, address the following issues:

- Do the rules actually represent the views of all three people in the group?
- How would the non-speakers have changed the rules if they could?
- How did the non-speakers feel during the actual exercise?
- Did the law maker remember to consult fully with the non-speakers?
- To what extent was the exercise a useful analogy for how the government of any country works?

Coursework

1 *'A study of public perceptions of crime within a given community'*
Focus on a small area and ask people which crimes they think actually occur most within that community. This data could then be compared with official police statistics on the occurrence of crime. Official statistics are usually related to police divisions and your local police force can explain to you how crime data is collected and may offer you data. Check this material is available before you begin any work. You may find that people have massive misconceptions and preconceptions about the amount and type of crime that takes place within their communities.

2 *'A qualitative study of the victims of crimes against property in a given local area'*
You are not sufficiently experienced to study victims of crimes against the person, such as rape or violence. Instead, gather information about how property crime impacts on people's lives. What do they feel about damage to property? To what extent is their emotional reaction linked to the actual damage caused or to the feelings that the crime has aroused in them? Which is more important, monetary value or the emotional values that we place on property?

Revision Hints

Knowledge is of less significance than analysis and evaluation in the final examination, so be sure that you understand the issues that have been raised in this chapter. If you do not, then return to the chapter on a regular basis. Your teacher is there to help, so ask for advice if necessary.

Be certain that you understand the following points:

* There is a difference between social codes and legal codes.
* Legal codes vary over time, place and culture.
* Legal codes represent mainly the beliefs of those in authority.
* Social codes are individual and cultural concepts.
* Deviance is a concept familiar to all cultures, though what constitutes deviance is culturally variable.
* It can be argued that crime is a social construct and is, therefore, a product of the society that labels an act as criminal and/or deviant.
* Sociologists vary according to their perspective in the way that they define and study crime.

Exam Hints

The significance of the material in this chapter to the study of crime and deviance cannot be overstated and the understanding that you have gained should underpin all of your thinking and writing about crime and deviance.

You could practise evaluation work by considering some of the following points and ideas related to the chapter. You are advised to brainstorm and record a series of ideas and judgements based around the following questions. Remember that there are no straightforward answers and a variety of points will give you the practice that you need in making judgements. When you have read the book, return to these questions and see if your responses still remain the same. The first three questions should make you think about the ways in which different cultures may impose different laws, a concept known as cultural relativity. The final three questions test your understandings of the concepts that you have been introduced to.

1 Alcohol is an addictive poison and should therefore be governed by the same rules as other dangerous drugs.
2 Prostitution should be legalised and taxed.
3 Smacking children should be made illegal in Britain.
4 There is no such thing as right and wrong; it depends on who you are and where you live.
5 The government determines crime but other people determine deviance.
6 The only laws we need are the Ten Commandments.

3

MEASURING CRIME

Introduction

IN THIS CHAPTER, we examine the various sources of information available to researchers who wish to explore the nature and extent of crime in society. There are three main sources of data used by sociologists and each will be examined in turn:

- official statistics
- victimisation studies
- self-report studies.

It is important to pay particular attention to the advantages and disadvantages of each source for studying the problem of crime in our society. Using these sources, it is possible to examine two particular areas, 'who is at risk of crime?' and 'who is afraid of crime?' These two groups are not necessarily the same people.

OFFICIAL CRIME STATISTICS

All countries gather detailed crime statistics. The key publication for crime figures in England and Wales is *Criminal Statistics*, the annual compilation of data produced by the Home Office. The data is derived from police and court records. Separate publications exist relating to Scotland and Northern Ireland, and are produced by the Scottish Office and the Northern Ireland Office.

Table 2: *Theorists, concepts and issues in this chapter*		
SOURCES OF DATA	KEY CONCEPTS	ISSUES TO CONSIDER
Official statistics	Tabulated data	How valid and reliable are official statistics?
Victimisation studies (National)	The dark figure of crime	To what extent is crime hidden from official statistics, ie unreported or unrecorded?
Victimisation studies (Local)	Left realism Locality studies Fear of crime	Levels of victimisation and fear of crime are affected by social divisions and area of residence.
Victimisation studies (Feminist)	Feminist perspectives Hidden crimes against women	Surveys informed by a feminist perspective reveal greater victimisation against women than national and local surveys.
Victimisation studies (International)	Comparative data	Levels of victimisation and fear of crime vary between different countries.
Self-report studies.	Hidden crime	Many crimes remain hidden because they are not reported, not recorded or no-one is aware they have been committed.

Activity

Increasingly, official statistics can be accessed using the Internet and you are advised to explore the Internet to obtain statistics from other countries.

At the time of writing, the Home Office Web site offers crime statistics for England and Wales: http://www.homeoffice.gov.uk

Try to find statistics for other countries. Entering 'crime' and 'statistics' or 'data' as key words for the search engine will be effective.

The analysis of official statistics gathered from a variety of countries has been influential in the development of sociology itself. The classical study which established a tradition of using data obtained from government agencies for research purposes is *Suicide* by **Emile Durkheim**. You should therefore use many of the issues raised in this chapter to develop your understanding of the discussion in Chapter 7, in which Durkheim's work on suicide is discussed in depth. One of the difficulties of using official crime statistics to make international comparisons is that not all societies gather crime statistics in exactly the same way. Moreover, activities are not equally criminal in all societies. Gun carrying is legal in the USA but a very serious offence in the Britain.

Activity
List all possible sources of data for crime statistics. Be imaginative in your consideration of who might actually be collecting information and for what purposes.

Criminal statistics (Home Office 1998) tell us that in 1997, the police recorded approximately 4.6 million offences in England and Wales. The majority of these offences relate to property crimes (91 per cent in 1997).

Table 3: *Criminal Offences recorded in 1997 (Home Office 1998)*	
OFFENCE GROUP	NUMBER (TO THE NEAREST 1,000)
Theft and handling stolen goods	2,165,000
Burglary	1,015,000
Criminal damage	877,000
Violence (including robbery)	314,000
Fraud and forgery	134,000
Sexual offences	33,000
Other notifiable offences	60,000
Total	**4,598,000**

Study point
1   Refer to Table 3. Which types of crimes were most likely to be reported to the police?
2   Can you suggest any reasons why car crime is more likely to be reported to the police than sexual offences?
3   Can you suggest reasons why fraud and forgery crimes are likely to be under-represented in the official figures?
4   What types of crime might come under the category of 'other'?

The statistics shown in Table 3 refer to offences recorded by the police in 1997 (Home Office 1998) but they only refer to offences about which the police are required to notify the Home Office. In the main, these are those crimes serious enough to be tried in a Crown Court. The less serious offences, which could only be tried in Magistrate's Courts, are missing.

Also absent are crimes committed which are recorded by agencies other than the police. Such agencies include the British Transport Police, Ministry of Defence Police, the Inland Revenue, Customs and Excise and the Department of Social Security. Consequently, the publication *Criminal Statistics*, even as a detailed record of criminal offences officially known to government bodies, is an incomplete picture of the extent of crime in England and Wales.

ANALYSING TRENDS

Statistics on crime have been collected since the mid-nineteenth century and so can provide some insight into trends in crime. They reveal that the overall crime rate in England and Wales, with the exception of small decreases in the 1950s, has risen every year since records began. Recently, this trend has been reversed. Official crime statistics from 1993 to 1997 have recorded consecutive falls in the crime rate.

However, you should be aware that analysing trends is more problematic than it first appears for a number of reasons:

- An increase in crime may be due to more crime being reported rather than more crime committed.
- Changes in law enforcement and the acts that are regarded as criminal make it difficult to determine historical increases and decreases in crime.
- Trends in particular kinds of crime may be moving in different directions in any one period. At present, levels of property crime seem to be falling and 'personal' crime rising.

Study point

Suggest reasons why people may be more willing to report crimes against the person and less willing to report property crimes to the police now than in the past.

Points of evaluation

1 The problem with using official statistics to analyse trends in crime illustrates a wider concern amongst sociologists: should we view official crime statistics as a product constructed by criminal justice agencies? This perspective is associated with Marxist and interactionist analyses. It is argued that official

crime statistics do not reflect the whole picture but only crime which is discovered, reported to the police and recorded by the police.

2 Moreover, official statistics only refer to acts that have been deemed criminal by the State (see Chapter 2).

3 This form of crime analysis shows that crime data may not be value-free and can be highly political in intent.

THE PRODUCTION OF OFFICIAL CRIME STATISTICS

Crime comes to the attention of the police in a number of ways. The police themselves detect relatively few offences as they are taking place. Their presence is likely to act as a deterrent to criminal activity. Instead, the police rely on the public to report offences after the actual event has occurred. However, many crimes will not be reported to the police. **Muncie** (1996) offers the following reasons:

- There may be ignorance that a crime has been committed (eg fraud).
- There appears to be no victim (eg prostitution).
- The offence may be considered trivial by the victim or observer (eg minor vandalism).
- The victim is powerless (eg child abuse).
- The victim distrusts the police and is concerned that the offence will not be taken seriously (eg sexual violence, particularly where the evidence is not especially clear-cut, such as date rape).
- The victim has no faith that the police will aim to protect his or her interests and fears reprisals if they report the offence (eg racial victimisation).

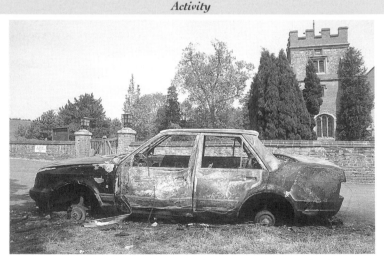

Activity

Car crime is almost always reported to the police. Can you suggest why this is so?

A wide range of personal and social factors influence whether incidents are reported to the police. Crucially, it depends on whether the observer perceives and interprets the behaviour as criminal. There are also practical considerations. For example, car theft is very likely to be reported because of the need to report the offence in order to receive payment from the insurance company.

Activity
Interview people around you to discover if they have ever been the victim of a crime which they did not report. Ask them to offer a reason why they did not report the crime. Offer a simple analysis of your results.

Once a crime has been reported there is no guarantee that the offence will end up as a crime statistic. In order to become a crime statistic, the offence has to be recorded by the police. The police have considerable discretion in this respect and practices vary between police forces. For instance, a study conducted in 1981 (Farrington and Dowds 1985) compared crime rates in Nottinghamshire with two similar counties. They found that the high crime rate in Nottinghamshire was because the police recorded all theft regardless of the value of the goods stolen and recorded all offences admitted by offenders to be taken into consideration. In addition, they counted multiple, continuous or series offences as separate crimes. The police also make decisions about the classification of offences. For example, attempted break-ins may be regarded as burglary in some areas and criminal damage in others.

Consequently, official crime statistics do not present us with the full picture. Yet they are revealing about public and police practices and priorities in relation to the problem of crime.

THE 'DARK FIGURE' OF CRIME

It is a commonly held view that official criminal statistics only represent 'the tip of the iceberg'.

Activity
1   What factors would affect whether a crime is reported to the police or not?
2   What factors will cause the police to respond to the crime?
3   What factors will determine whether the police will record the crime?

The 'dark figure' refers to the vast number of unrecorded crimes that do not appear in official statistics. If we are to get some sense of the nature and extent of the dark figure, we need to use alternative sources of data. We can collect statistical data in two main ways:

1 Victimisation studies involve asking individuals about their experiences of crime.
2 Self-report studies involve asking individuals to reveal to a researcher their offending behaviour.

VICTIMISATION STUDIES

Victimisation studies operate on three levels: national, local and international. All use a quantitative approach, collecting statistical data by means of questionnaires. We will explore each of these different types of surveys in turn.

National surveys

National crime surveys have a number of strengths. They enable researchers to estimate the extent of the dark figure of crime and also provide data on the public's reporting habits. The British Crime Survey began reporting in 1982 and the 1998 report is the seventh survey (although at the time of writing the data has yet to be fully analysed). The latest 'sweep' is based on interviews with almost 15,000 adults aged 16 or over. Respondents were asked to give details of crimes in which they had been a victim during the last 12 months.

The 1998 survey (Mirrlees-Black *et al* 1998) estimates that a total of nearly 16.5 million crimes were committed in 1997, of which only 44 per cent were reported to the police. Of these only 54 per cent were recorded by the police. The 1998 survey was the first time a fall had been recorded and it confirms the downward trend in recorded crime. However, the study of crime rates over the 14-year period (until 1996) reveals a less steep increase in rates of crime than police figures suggest.

The data collected is more than a simple count of crime because it provides a detailed database on crime-related topics for policy-makers and researchers. It offers a basis for estimating the extent of the dark figure of crime and tells us which crimes occur and where they occur. There are numerous studies based on British Crime Survey data including studies of racially motivated crime, drug abuse and fear of crime.

Points of evaluation

National crime surveys can be criticised in a number of ways. **Coleman** and **Moynihan** (1996) suggest a number of questions we need to ask when examining this type of data:

1 Is the sample representative? Does it reflect who lives in the country being studied?

2 How accurately will people remember what has happened to them?
3 Do people tell the truth?
4 Is it possible that some groups of respondents are more likely to report being a victim of crime than other people?
5 Is it possible that different groups of people may view the same act in different ways?
6 How compatible are people's definitions of crime with legal definitions?

One main problem with national surveys is that they tend to reduce the experience of crime to some mythical 'average' person which glosses over some of the most significant differences in risk of victimisation. For example, the British Crime Survey (Hough and Mayhew 1983) found that the statistically average person aged 16 or over can expect:

- a robbery once every five centuries (not attempts)
- an assault resulting in injury (even if slight) once every century
- a family car to be stolen or taken once every 60 years
- a burglary in the home once every 40 years.

We know from our own experiences that certain people can expect to experience significantly greater levels of crime than the average, depending upon a variety of personal and social factors, such as where they live. This is confirmed by data from local crime surveys.

Activity
Ask people if they feel that the possibility of being a victim of crime limits their activities. Are there differences in responses linked to age, gender and ethnicity?

Local surveys

Local crime surveys have been carried out in response to some of the perceived inadequacies of national surveys. By focusing on particular localities, these surveys attempted to pinpoint the higher levels of fear prevailing in socially deprived inner city areas and the disproportionate amount of victimisation experienced by particular social groups. An example of a local survey is the Islington Crime Survey (Jones *et al* 1986). Islington is an inner city area in London (at the time the survey was conducted it was the seventh most deprived area in England). The researchers found higher levels of victimisation, in particular, high levels of multiple victimisation amongst women, ethnic minorities and the poor. A startling statistic is that burglary, robbery or sexual assault had touched a third of all households within the previous 12 months.

If you were a potential burglar or a mugger considering a victim, what sort of signals would you look for from homes or people to show that targetting them would produce an easy profit? What can people do to avoid victim status?

This type of work is associated with a school of thought known as **left realism**. This school of thought describes itself as radical in its criminology but realistic in its appraisal of crime and its causes (Young 1997). It aims to take crime seriously, recognising that crime is a very real problem for a large section of the population, particularly women, the poor and ethnic minorities. This concern is coupled with a belief that crime has to be explored within its social context. Left realists suggest that we need to examine the causes of criminal acts and the response of agencies of social control. Chapter 9 explores this perspective in more detail.

Whilst most local surveys have focused on inner city areas, there are some examples of surveys conducted on rural areas. An example is the Aberystwyth (West Wales) Crime Survey (Koffman 1996). The data collected was compared to British Crime Survey data on Wales. The Aberystwyth Crime Survey found a different pattern of crime. In particular, it discovered lower levels of burglary and vehicle theft but higher levels of vandalism and damage to vehicles. Rural crime surveys are highly significant in that they challenge the view that crime is primarily an urban problem and they recognise that some types of crime are highly prevalent in rural areas.

You will almost certainly find a branch of the Victim Support Group in your local area. The police station or a telephone directory are probably the best places to find a contact address and number. Victim Support will not give you names and addresses of victims of crime as their service is confidential. They may be able to tell you about overall local patterns of referral and individual responses to crime.

Feminist researchers have carried out a number of studies of personal crimes (Hanmer and Saunders 1984, Hall 1985). These surveys suggest the level of sexual crime against women is far higher than that revealed by national victim surveys and infinitely higher than that indicated by police records. This can largely be attributed to the sensitivity of feminist survey questions and the approach and demeanour of the interviewers. It is probable that victims will feel more comfortable with the researcher, and the researcher and the victim are more likely to have shared views on what might be regarded as a criminal act.

International surveys

The latest international survey (Home Office 1996) compares victimisation rates for 11 countries. These included England and Wales, Northern Ireland, Scotland, six European Nations, Canada and the USA. Overall rises were higher than average in England and Wales, average in Scotland and below average in Northern Ireland. Comparisons between survey data and police crime figures show similar trends in most countries for the period 1988–95.

Table 4 shows the percentage of the population experiencing victimisation once or more overall, and for three different offences. Contact crime refers to robbery, assaults with force and sexual assaults (against women only).

Table 4: *Percentage of the population in different countries experiencing victimisation in 1996 (Home Office 1998)*				
COUNTRY	OVERALL	CONTACT CRIME*	THEFT OF A CAR	BURGLARY OR ATTEMPTS
England and Wales	31	3.6	3.0	6.1
Northern Ireland	17	1.5	1.9	2.5
Scotland	26	2.7	2.2	3.6
Austria	19	1.6	0.2	1.3
Finland	19	2.9	0.6	1.2
France	25	2.2	1.8	3.9
Netherlands	31	1.9	0.4	5.1
Sweden	24	3.4	1.5	2.0
Switzerland	24	3.4	1.5	2.0
USA	24	3.5	2.1	4.9
Canada	25	2.7	1.7	5.3

*Robbery, assaults with force and sexual assaults (against women only).

Activity

Look at Table 4:

1 Beginning with the country with the greatest overall risk of victimisation, put the countries in rank order.
2 Repeat this for contact crime, theft of a car and burglary or attempts.
3 Compare your four lists.
4 Suggest reasons why we should treat the data in the table with caution.

SELF-REPORT STUDIES

Self-report studies were first used in the USA in the 1940s. More recently, they have been used in international comparative work. In these studies, ordinary members of the public are asked to report their own criminal acts.

Activity
Assess the criminality of members of your group, school or college. Ask respondents to reveal (anonymously) what criminal acts they have committed within the past year. Are there differences in gender or religious affiliation patterns? How reliable are your results? Write a 500-word report.

Although adding an additional dimension to the official picture, these studies can be criticised on a number of grounds.

Points of evaluation

1 Self-report studies tend to focus on trivial misbehaviour rather than serious criminal acts.
2 We can also question the validity of the data. We might argue that people are unwilling to report their criminal acts. Alternatively, we could suggest that some groups might exaggerate their levels of offending, believing it enhances their status.
3 Often these studies have focused only on the self-reported offending of lower-class urban adolescent males.

Thus, the most fundamental limitation of self-report studies is that they do not tell us about the serious, but hidden, crimes of adults. All self-report studies suggest that a vast amount of petty crime is carried out and that few of the perpetrators are ever caught or involved in the justice system in any way.

FEAR OF CRIME

Victimisation studies also cover the issue of fear of crime. Increasingly, criminologists have become aware that the fear of crime is a social problem in its own right. Fears about crime have great consequences and can significantly alter the way in which people live their lives.

One of the questions asked in the British Crime Survey is 'How safe do you feel when walking alone in this area after dark?' The findings reveal that older women tend to be the most afraid and that younger men – who are most likely to end up as a victim in a violent or other criminal incident on the street – are the least likely to admit fear. Based on these findings, some commentators and many politicians argue that the fears of elderly women are irrational because they do not reflect the 'reality' of crime figures.

Criticisms of the suggestion that fear of crime is irrational have come in particular from feminists and left realists who make the following points:

- Firstly, young men may be unwilling to own up to fear outside at night because in British society one of the key characteristics of masculinity is being seen to be 'tough'.
- Secondly, fear of crime is not just about the chance of being victimised but about the consequences. People can, and do, worry about things which are unlikely to happen but which would be very distressing if they did. To illustrate, the consequences of a serious assault are far greater for elderly women than young men.
- Thirdly, elderly women are perhaps less likely to be the victims of street crime because their fear constrains their lifestyles.

Table 5: *Fear of crime by gender and age (British Crime Survey 1996) – percentage of people 'very worried' about theft of a car, burglary and rape*						
TYPE OF CRIME	MALES AGED 16–29	MALES AGED 30–59	MALES AGED 60+	FEMALE AGED 16–29	FEMALE AGED 30–59	FEMALES AGED 60+
Theft of a car*	28	23	19	30	26	22
Burglary	18	18	18	27	26	25
Rape	–	–	–	44	31	22

*Car owners only.

Activity
1 Suggest reasons why young males are more likely to fear the loss of a car more than other types of crime.
2 Which crime are females most in fear of? Is this fear realistic?
3 For which crime are age differences in levels of fear less marked?
4 The survey only asks women about their fear of rape. However, given that male rape does actually occur, perhaps the survey should also ask men this question. Do you think many males would admit to fear of rape?

Again national surveys only tell us about the average person. Fear of crime is highest in areas where levels of victimisation are highest. A local crime survey may be better placed to capture the relationship between fear of crime and risk of victimisation. For example, the Islington Crime Survey found higher levels of fear than average in contrast to the Aberystwyth survey which found anxiety about crime in this rural area to be lower than average.

Women report the highest levels of fear of crime but conversely, men are much more at risk of becoming victims of violence. However, we can understand more fully the fears of women if we explore their vulnerability in the home and in the street. For women, their fear is often particular types of crime such as rape, even though its actual occurrence is relatively rare. Women will constrain their lives in ways as to limit the possibilities of this type of crime occurring. Crime prevention literature often suggests women should behave in particular ways, especially after dark such as not using public transport, moving in groups or avoiding open spaces.

Activity
Few women are fully open with males about the varieties and frequency of sexual harassment or gender-related insults they experience at some points in their lives. If females in the group are willing, then individuals could write down some of their actual experiences in such a way as to remain anonymous and non-aggressive. Word processing is useful for this. Use these notes as the basis for discussion as to whether female fear of rape or sexual attack is, in fact, realistic.

An interesting paradox which emerges from feminist surveys is that women, especially young women, report being very worried about rape by strangers, but have less fear of violence by known men. This is despite the fact that they are probably more at risk from men they know. This may reflect popular conceptions that the streets are 'dangerous' and the home is 'safe'. It may also reflect the way that crime is depicted, with sensationalised fictional and non-fictional stories of stranger rapists and killers being the focus of much television coverage and newspaper reporting. This type of stranger crime is far more rare than the typical sex-crime scenario, where a woman is most likely to be raped by an acquaintance or a relative in her or his own home.

Like national and local surveys, international surveys are also revealing about fear of crime. Fear of crime varies between individuals in different countries. People in England and Wales were more likely than those in any other country to think they would be burgled in the next 12 months. Based on the latest available data (1992) 10 per cent thought it was very likely that they would be burgled. The lowest levels of fear were reported in Finland where only 1 per cent thought it was very likely they would be burgled in the next 12 months (cited in Social Trends 1997).

SUMMARY

Despite the availability of other sources of data about crime, official criminal statistics remain the 'barometer of crime' (Maguire 1997) used by politicians and highlighted in the media. Statements such as 'Crime soars out of control' and 'Police lose the fight against crime' are typical newspaper headlines. It is important not to lose sight of the value of official statistics, but we should approach them with caution. The true facts about crime are probably unknowable, but by combining different data sources we can at least get a fuller picture of the nature and extent of crime in society through revealing some of the dark figure of crime. Additionally, one of the key contributions of other data sources has been to put a concern with fear of crime on the criminological agenda, thus examining one of the far-reaching but little explored effects of crime in society.

Table 6: *Summary of research methods*		
DATA SOURCE	STRENGTHS	WEAKNESSES
Official statistics	1 Easy to obtain from published texts. 2 Detailed information on crimes and criminals. 3 Allow cautious study of trends over time.	1 They do not tell us about the nature of the dark figure. 2 Not all crimes reported to the police are recorded. 3 They may tell us more about police practices than the extent of crime.
Victim studies	1 Offer the possibility of discovering at least some of the dark figure of crime. 2 If handled sensitively, they can be used to find out about crimes rarely reported to the police. 3 Allow analysis of patterns of victimisation and fear of crime.	1 Reliable information about victimisation may not be obtained from respondents. 2 Time-consuming to conduct especially at a national or international level. 3 Respondents may be unwilling to report their fears about crime.
Self-report studies	1 'From the horse's mouth.' 2 Offer triangulation for other sources of data and provides detail on offenders.	1 Bravado on part of respondents who may exaggerate. 2 People do not own up to serious crimes.

STUDY GUIDES

Key Concept Activity

Look at the following terms and be sure that you understand their meaning. Use them in your examination work:

- the dark figure of crime
- victim survey
- self-report studies
- left realism.

Group Work

1   As a group, compare official statistics for truancy and non-attendance in your institution with a self-report study of truancy. Which form of study gave you the most accurate data in your view?

2   In your groups, collect a selection of local and national newspapers. With marker pens, circle the stories that deal with criminal acts. Which crimes are most reported in the papers? Which crimes are least reported? What type of language is used to describe the acts in the reporting of crime? In your view, is there any relationship between the crimes that people fear and the way that crime is reported in newspapers?

Coursework

1   *'A Study of Responses to Victimisation'*
    Using in-depth interviews, talk to people you know who have been the victim of a property crime, such as burglary, criminal damage or car theft. Discuss their feelings and responses to what has occurred. Does their response vary according to the severity of the crime in your view or are there other factors involved?

2   *'An Analysis of the Relationship Between Fear of Crime and Risk of Crime'*
    You will need to be fairly sophisticated in your ability to use statistical data for this exercise. Collect information about the incidence of crime in your locality or the incidence of crime nationally. Collect information about a sample of people in terms of gender, ethnicity, age and social class. If relevant, you should also consider degree of mental or physical ability. Now ask your sample to rank crimes in terms of their fear of or belief that they could be the victims of this type of crime. The final step is to consider how 'realistic' their fears are in terms of the statistical occurrence of those crimes for people with similar social characteristics to themselves. A simpler version would be to restrict your sample to members of a fairly homogenous social group such as

female pensioners or college students. Is there a close relationship between the fear of crime and the statistical likelihood of a person becoming a victim?

Revision Hints

Ensure that you are familiar with some actual findings and statistical data so that you can quote effectively under examination conditions. Spend some time with copies of *Social Trends* and *Criminal Statistics*.

Collect a cuttings file of crime reports from newspapers. You should focus on the actual debates around crimes rather than just the reports of the crimes. This should give you plenty of case study evidence to use in support of your arguments. Make sure that you have notes in order to answer the following questions:

1 What difficulties exist for sociologists who rely on officially collected data?
2 In what ways might victim studies prove to be more reliable than official statistics in the recording of personal crimes such as rape?
3 Suggest ethical and practical difficulties a sociologist might expect to experience when designing and conducting a self-report study.

Exam Hints

1 *Evaluate the usefulness of official police figures for an understanding of the occurrence of crime in our society.*

   Some variation of this question is the most frequently asked on this topic in any examination, and so you are advised to read the chapter very thoroughly and to make sure that you understand the issues. The debate has far wider implications than an illustration of your understanding of crime data and its collection, because empirical research is at the heart of the discipline of sociology. You should draw significant conclusions about the nature of the methodology of social science itself. Are 'scientifically' collected official data reliable? Does data which is based on people's interpretations of events actually reflect the reality of their society? The evaluations should be your own and reflect some very deep thinking on your part as to the value of official data. Both an outright rejection of or an uncritical acceptance of official data will score very low marks.

2 Substitute a different data source for *police figures* in the above question and practise answering this exam-style question.

4

PATTERNS OF CRIME AND CRIMINAL BEHAVIOUR

Introduction

CHAPTER 3 INTRODUCED you to the various sources of data available to sociologists who wish to explore patterns of crime and criminal behaviour. In this chapter, we will use these official and unofficial data sources to discuss the social characteristics of offenders, focusing on age, gender, social class, ethnicity; and also consider the distribution of crime across areas.

Throughout the chapter, we are concerned with two key questions:

- What is known and what is not known about the social characteristics of offenders?
- Official statistics suggest that the typical offender is young, male, black and lower class. How far is this an accurate portrayal?

Activity
Ask a number of people to give you 10 words which describe how you would recognise a criminal. Certain words and phrases will be repeated by nearly everyone.
What do the findings tell you about popular perceptions of the criminal and the social construction of crime in society?

Table 7: *Theorists, concepts and issues in this chapter*		
KEY THEORISTS	KEY CONCEPTS	KEY ISSUES
Farrington	Age Criminal career	Crime is disproportionately committed by young people.
Heidensohn	Gender	Women commit a small share of all crimes.
Marxist criminologists	Social class Hidden crimes of the powerful eg white-collar crime	Convicted offenders are usually working class but this may reflect biases in criminal law and criminal justice.
Smith	Ethnicity	Black people are disproportionately represented among convicted offenders but this may be the result of discrimination in the criminal justice system.
Chicago School (Park, Burgess, Shaw, McKay) Environmental criminologists (Bottoms, Wikstrom)	Social geography	Crime is concentrated in particular areas of the city.

AGE

Young people are disproportionately represented amongst known offenders. Official crime statistics suggest that crime is overwhelmingly committed by adolescents who increasingly offend up to a peak age and then gradually give up crime after a relatively short criminal career. The peak age for offending by females and males is 18 (Home Office 1998). Until recently no criminal conviction was possible for anyone under the age of 10 years because that is the age at which children are deemed to understand the difference between 'naughtiness' and 'serious wrong' in the eyes of the law. This is no longer the case following the introduction of recent legislation, the Crime and Disorder Act 1998.

Look at Table 8. It gives the number of young offenders (in 1,000s) found guilty by either the Youth Court (10–17-year-olds) or Magistrates' or Crown Court (17–21-year-olds), or cautioned by the police for the four commonest types of crimes in 1997 (Home Office 1998). The number of offenders is broken down by gender and age.

Table 8: *Numbers of young offenders (1,000s) by type of crime in 1997 (Home Office 1998)*					
OFFENCE	MALES AGED 10–14	MALES AGED 14–18	MALES AGED 18–21	FEMALES AGED 10–14	FEMALES AGED 14–18	FEMALES AGED 18–21
Theft and handling stolen goods	9.7	33.9	23.3	4.6	12.3	6.8
Drug offences	0.3	10.4	19.5	0.0	0.9	1.8
Violence against the person	1.8	10.3	7.6	0.6	2.8	1.0
Burglary	3.3	11.9	7.6	0.2	0.7	0.3
All indictable offences*	17.0	78.7	73.6	5.7	18.7	12.0

*Indictable offences are offences which can be tried at the Crown Court although proceedings will commence in the Magistrates' Court. These are the most serious crimes.

Activity

Look at Table 8 and answer the following questions:

1 What was the total number of convictions for males aged between 10 and 21 in 1997?
2 What was the total number of convictions for females aged between 10 and 21 in 1997?
3 In what way does the pattern for drug-related convictions among offenders differ from that of other crime convictions?
4 For which type of crime are males most likely to receive a conviction?
5 How many more times is a male likely to be convicted of a drug-related crime than a female?
6 At what age is a person most likely to gain a criminal conviction?

Whilst the relationship between age and crime is often referred to as one of the few facts agreed upon by criminological researchers, we can think of ways in which official criminal statistics may overemphasise the crimes of the young:

- The crimes of young people are more likely to be detected because young people are subject to the control and surveillance of agencies such as schools and the family.
- Young offenders are more likely to carry out their crimes in groups and in public places and thus are more likely to be detected.
- In contrast, crimes committed by adults are more likely to remain hidden. Such crimes might include domestic violence, child abuse and white-collar crime.

However, other sources of data suggest that levels of offending amongst young people may be even higher than official criminal statistics indicate. The Youth Lifestyles Survey commissioned by the Home Office provided information on the self-reported offending behaviour of young people in England and Wales in 1992–3. They found that one in four males aged 18–21 and around one in eight females aged 14–17 admitted committing theft or burglary in the previous year (cited in *Social Trends* 1997). The Cambridge Study of Delinquent Development (Farrington 1997) also enables us to compare patterns of offending at different ages. This is a longitudinal study of 400 working-class boys from South London born in 1953 who have been followed up at regular intervals from the age of eight years. Self-report questionnaires were used to discover the criminal behaviour of these young men. By the age of 32, 96 per cent of the men had committed at least one of the 10 specified offences (including burglary, theft, assault, vandalism and drug use), most committing offences in their teenage years. However, when analysing the findings of this study, it is difficult to separate the influence of age on offending behaviour from the effect of gender and social class. All these factors are relevant to the study of criminal behaviour.

Study point
Is it possible that the police use the same stereotypes and assumptions as the rest of us? Do members of your group know of, or have experiences of, the police or security guards in shops, stopping or following young people?

GENDER

Official criminal statistics give us a picture of men, rather than women, behaving badly. Based on the data for 1997, for every woman found guilty in the Crown Court on a serious charge (indictable offences), there were almost seven men. For the less serious offences (summary offences), men were found guilty more than twice as often as women. The most common types of offences committed by both women and men are property offences but there are some important gender differences.

Activity
List what you think are probably 'typical' female crimes. Ask others around you to suggest what they consider to be female crimes. Compare these results with the conviction figures. How accurate are people's perceptions?

Men are 10 times more likely than women to be found guilty of:

- sexual offences
- violent offences
- burglary
- motoring offences
- robbery
- criminal damage.

There are only two offences that women are more likely to be convicted of. These are:

- TV licence evasion
- offence by a prostitute.

Study point
Suggest reasons why women are more likely than men to be convicted of TV licence evasion and offence by a prostitute.

However, whilst women's crimes are usually less serious, we should not lose sight of the fact that women are involved in all types of crime including the most serious offences, such as murder and sexual offences. However, the gender ratio is very startling and holds true for many countries and over time. We need to ask why women's crime rates are so low and conversely why men's are so high? We will consider possible explanations in Chapters 5 and 6.

Points of evaluation

The problem of relying on official criminal statistics to explore the relationship between gender and crime are two-fold.

Firstly, official criminal statistics are the product of police and court processes and there is evidence that women and men receive differential treatment in the criminal justice system. It appears at first glance that women are treated more leniently by the police. They are more likely to be cautioned (ie given a formal warning), but this can be explained by the less serious nature of their offences. They are also less likely to be stopped and searched, but only a small percentage of stops actually result in arrests. Studies suggest differential treatment by the courts, but there is a lack of conclusive evidence of systematic discrimination (Hedderman and Hough 1994). However, there is evidence to suggest that particular groups of women who do not conform to gender stereotypes are treated more harshly by the police (Horn, 1995) and by the courts (Carlen, 1983; Eaton 1986). This might include violent women, women who are perceived as bad mothers or women who are prostitutes.

Secondly, official criminal statistics do not tell us about hidden crime. We need to ask is the dark figure female or male? The dark figure of crime is a term used to describe all of the criminal activities which do not appear in official statistics. **Pollak** (1961) suggests that women's crimes are masked and convicted female offenders represent only the tip of a very large iceberg. He views women as innately deceitful and suggests that in their domestic roles they have numerous opportunities to commit and conceal crime. This view is clearly based on stereotypical assumptions and it is difficult to find evidence to support his view. Undoubtedly, a significant proportion of crimes committed by women are not discovered and thus do not appear in official criminal statistics. Other sources of data such as victimisation surveys are not revealing about the gender of offenders. However, it can reasonably be assumed that the dark figure involves crime committed by men, as well as women. For example, the crimes that are known to remain hidden, such as domestic violence, white-collar crime and organised crime, are more likely to be committed by men.

The exact ratio of male to female offending is unknowable but as **Heidensohn** (1997) notes, three main trends and patterns in female criminality have long been observed:

1 Women commit a small share of all crimes.
2 Women's crimes are fewer, less serious, more rarely professional and less likely to be repeated.
3 Women are represented in very small numbers in the prison population (between 4 and 5 per cent in England and Wales).

SOCIAL CLASS

There is a well-established link between social class and crime that has been of particular concern to Marxist sociologists (see Chapters 5 and 6). For Marxists, social class is defined by relationship to the means of production and society can be broadly divided into two classes: the bourgeoisie (who own the means of production) and the proletariat (who work for the bourgeoisie). However, criminological researchers have used a number of measures of class including occupational status, income and housing. Occupational status is the most commonly used.

Official criminal statistics do not provide information on the social class of offenders but some insight can be gained from the National Prison Survey (Walmsley et al 1992) which classified prisoners based on their most recent employment prior to imprisonment. This data suggested that the lower social classes were disproportionately represented in the prison population. However, we should be wary of relying on this data alone for the reasons discussed below.

Points of evaluation

- This data only tells us about the social class of known offenders who have been convicted and imprisoned.
- Using employment status to determine social class is problematic because of high levels of unemployment in the work histories of prisoners.
- More fundamentally, we could argue that crimes committed by offenders of the lower social classes are more likely to come to the attention of the criminal justice system. To illustrate, research has shown that those engaged in benefit fraud are more likely to be detected and prosecuted than those involved in tax evasion (Cook 1989).
- We could also argue that the criminal justice system responds in different ways to offenders from different social classes. For example, drunken behaviour in the inner city may be defined in terms of disorder but the same behaviour by middle-class students may be defined in terms of 'high spirits'.

The study of the relationship between social class and crime is more complex than sociologists of crime and deviance initially assumed. Increasingly we have become aware of the involvement of individuals from the higher social classes in white-collar crime. Similarly, the relationship between ethnicity and crime is also a complex one.

ETHNICITY

Our starting point must be a definition of what sociologists refer to as ethnicity since this is so commonly confused with race. Whilst the term race has been used to refer to the view that humans can be categorised by physical characteristics ethnicity defines groups with reference to shared culture, language, customs and institutions. Ethnicity allows for consideration of the different life experiences of different ethnic groups. This is of particular relevance to those studying crime and deviance because, whilst black people (those of African and Caribbean origin) have a disproportionately high crime rate, we find lower levels of offending amongst the Asian population.

In 1993, the 10-yearly census conducted in Britain included a question on ethnic origin for the first time. There were nine categories to choose from, or people could define themselves. It was found that only 5.5 per cent of the population of Britain belonged to an ethnic minority. Data is not available on the ethnic origins of people who become officially defined as offenders, although police forces do keep records of the ethnic origin of those arrested. For example, the Metropolitan Police Department categorise arrest rates according to skin colour and suggest that those classified as black make up a disproportionate number of arrests, especially for street robbery of personal property. This might be more revealing about who police officers in the Metropolitan Police regard as the usual suspects than about black people's involvement in crime.

The Prison Service routinely collect data on the ethnic origins of prisoners. The data reveals that black people are disproportionately represented among the prison population. We can explain this in two ways (Smith 1997):

1 Black people have a higher involvement in crime than other groups.
2 Black people are more likely to be drawn into, and less likely to be filtered out of, the criminal justice system.

We can argue that both these proportions are true. Black people may be more likely to be involved in crime given that the black population is younger and experiences greater social and economic disadvantage which may be related to discrimination in other areas of social life such as housing, education and employment. There is also evidence to suggest that discrimination occurs at different points of the criminal justice system. Black people are more likely to be:

- stopped by the police (Norris et al 1992)
- arrested (Smith and Gray 1985)
- sent for trial rather than cautioned (ie dealt with by the courts rather than the police) (Landau and Nathan 1983)
- remanded in custody (ie held in prison to await trial) (Hood 1992)
- tried at the Crown Court (ie tried by a Judge and Jury with greater sentencing powers (Brown and Hullin 1992)
- given a harsher sentence (Hood 1992).

Putting these two views together, Smith (1997) argues that a higher involvement by black people in crime produces stereotypes upon which discriminatory treatment is based. This leads to perceptions about the black crime rate rising, thus reinforcing stereotypes and discriminatory attitudes.

However, given the data we have, it is difficult to come to any clear conclusions about the relationship between ethnicity and crime. The situation is more complex when we explore the under-representation of Asians amongst the prison population. This group has arguably suffered from as much discrimination as other ethnic minorities.

Activity
Ask a variety of people to describe a drug dealer. How many of the assumptions that they make are based on issues of ethnicity, class, gender and age?

THE SOCIAL GEOGRAPHY OF CRIME

A concern with where offenders live dates back to the work of sociologists in the US of the 1920s at the University of Chicago. They embarked upon a systematic study of all aspects of their urban local environment.

Park et al divided the city into five areas:

Zone 1   Central business district (city centre)
Zone 2   Transition zone (area of economic deprivation, physical deterioration, population instability and cultural fragmentation – the inner city)
Zone 3   Working-class homes
Zone 4   Middle-class homes
Zone 5   Commuter suburbs

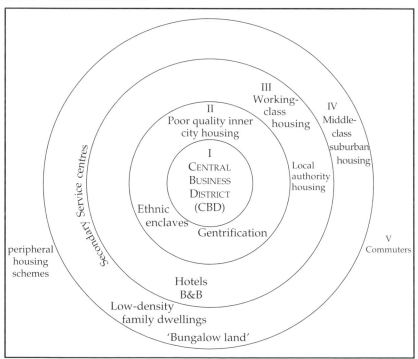

CONCENTRIC RINGS OF THE CHICAGO SCHOOL (DERIVED FROM **BURGESS**, 1925)

Park et al hypothesised that crime and deviance would flourish in Zone 2. **Shaw** and **McKay** (1942) used prison and court records of juvenile delinquents to test this view. Their observations were as follows:

- The closer to the city centre, the higher the rate of crime.
- High crime rates occurred in areas characterised by physical deterioration and declining populations.
- Relatively high crime rates persisted in Zone 2 even though the population was constantly changing.

From this they concluded that it was the nature of neighbourhoods, not the nature of individuals who lived there, that determined levels of criminality.

Points of evaluation

1 This view is very deterministic and suggests that anyone who lived in these areas would engage in offending behaviour. There is no room to consider individual motivations and social interactions. Later studies by the Chicago School developed this aspect.

2 The work of the Chicago School draws on court and prison records and thus ignores hidden crime such as white-collar crime (likely to be concentrated in Zone 1) and crimes within the family (likely to be concentrated in Zones 3, 4 and 5).

3 The work of the Chicago School tends to confuse offender-based data (where offenders live) and offence-based data (where offences are committed). As sociologists, we cannot assume that offenders commit crimes near to their homes. However, research shows that juveniles are more likely than their adult counterparts to commit crimes close to their homes.

Official crime data still continues to suggest that crime is concentrated in particular areas. It is almost universally agreed upon that crime rates are higher in urban areas. The city has traditionally been seen as a 'dangerous' place and more recently, there has been a criminological concern with 'hotspots' of crime (ie areas with disproportionately high rates of crime). These areas might include social housing estates, 'red light' areas and areas of the city where pubs and clubs are concentrated, and police surveillance is often targetted on these areas. Some light has also been shed on the areas where offenders live. Studies in cities as diverse as Sheffield, England (Baldwin and Bottoms 1976) and Stockholm, Sweden (Wikström 1991) suggest that known offenders tend to be concentrated in particular areas of the city, especially the most economically and socially deprived areas such as the inner city and areas of social housing. However, little support has been found for the zone model of the Chicago School. Recent work by environmental criminologists has explored both the spatial distribution of offences and offenders (see Bottoms and Wiles 1997).

Can you name local areas with reputations for high crime rates? Are these areas which are more likely to be inhabited by wealthy people or large numbers of poorer people? What activities take place in these areas?

SUMMARY

Official criminal statistics reveal a great deal about the social characteristics of offenders. The picture painted is that a disproportionate amount of crime is committed by young, lower-class males who live in particular areas of the city. The evidence on the ethnic origins of offenders is less clear-cut. However, we need to acknowledge that not all crime is reported and recorded. Official criminal statistics therefore may tell us more about who is being criminalised than who is criminal. We can only speculate on the social characteristics of those committing the dark figure of crime.

Key Concept Activity

Look at the following terms and be sure you understand their sociological meaning:

- gender
- ethnicity
- social class
- social geography.

Group Work

1 Ask a spokesperson from the local police station to visit and talk about patterns of crime in your local area.
2 Obtain data from the local police force or from your local authority. Analyse it carefully and see if any patterns emerge. Does crime appear to vary significantly between areas?

Coursework

'Females are more conformist than males'

Study females and males in a closed institution such as a school or a college and explore patterns of rule-breaking within the institution. Compare the trends that emerge and analyse them to see if there is a relationship between gender and severity of misdemeanour. This work could be developed by considering ethnicity or social class if the data is available. Be sure people would be willing to cooperate with your study before you begin.

Revision Hints

This is an enormously important part of the course and you should reread this chapter on a regular basis. An understanding of social inequality and social class is written into the syllabus requirements of all of the examining boards as a key social concept at A Level and you must therefore expect questions testing this knowledge. You should develop a view of what the official statistics offer us in terms of a picture of the 'typical' criminal and then list points that support or argue against the official statistics. This has been started for you below but you should finish the table for yourself as you reread the chapter.

Social Characteristics	Official Records	Points which support the official picture	Points which criticise the official picture
Age	Young people, 14 – 21 years, commit most crime	Courts are full of young people Self-report studies favour this view	Young are surveyed more Young can be stereotyped
Gender	Males appear to commit most crime		Women may receive differential treatment
Class	Working class commit most crime		
Ethnicity	The picture is muddled but Afro-Caribbean men seem to be over-represented		
Social geography	Crime is an inner city phenomena		

In addition, you are advised to summarise the views of significant writers in this particular debate and to attempt to locate them in their perspective. This is not an easy task all of the time, but certain clues may help:

- Marxists will think in terms of social class and social control.
- Functionalists will discuss shared values.
- Interactionists will look for meaning in action.
- Feminists are concerned with gender issues.

Exam Hints

Often stimulus questions are included which relate to the issues explored in this chapter. Make sure you have looked at and practised the activities based on analysing and interpreting crime data in this chapter, in addition to planning practice essays.

1 *Evaluate the suggestion that the typical criminal is a working-class adolescent male.*
   In your evaluation you should be aware that crime data should be approached with caution because it is a product of social processes, not simply a count of actual criminal behaviour. However, you would be unwise to reject the findings of official data altogether. Instead, you need to combine the insights which can be gleaned from official data with the findings of the research studies discussed in this chapter. Make sure you understand the different factors which may influence a person's likelihood of obtaining a criminal conviction.
2 Substitute ethnic minority for *working-class adolescent male* in question 1 and practice this exam-style question.

5

EXPLAINING CRIME AND DEVIANCE: THE DEVELOPMENTS OF SOCIOLOGICAL APPROACHES

Introduction

IT IS OFTEN assumed that, if we knew why people commit criminal acts, we would be able to solve the problem of crime. Consequently, the search for the causes of crime continues to occupy sociological, political and popular debate. Numerous explanations have been offered and we will consider some popular notions before rejecting them. Sociologists have offered a wide range of possibilities to explain both crime and deviance and the main perspectives are discussed in Chapters 5 and 6.

In this chapter, we will focus on the period up to the 1960s and chart the development of the sociology of crime and deviance. Functionalist, sub-cultural and early Marxist approaches are described and assessed. As you read through the chapters, you should evaluate these theories for yourself, paying particular attention to their ability to explain the patterns of crime outlined in the previous chapter.

THE DEVELOPMENT OF SOCIOLOGICAL EXPLANATIONS

Sociological explanations for the origins of crime have developed throughout the twentieth century and contrast greatly with earlier explanations of crime. Early explanations of criminal behaviour looked to the individual rather than society to explain this phenomena.

Table 9: *Theorists, concepts and issues in this chapter*			
KEY THEORIES	KEY THEORISTS	KEY CONCEPTS	KEY IDEAS
Functionalism	Durkheim Merton	Collective conscience Anomie/strain Normality/pathology	Crime is normal, inevitable and functional (Durkheim). Crime can be explained in terms of the social structure of society (Merton).
Sub-cultural approaches	Cohen Cloward and Ohlin	Sub-culture Delinquent values	Crime is normal behaviour within particular social groups.
Early Marxism	Bonger	Class struggle Exploitation Power White-collar crime	Crime can be explained in terms of the economic relations of capitalist society.

CLASSICISM

Beccaria (1764) developed one of the first formal explanations of criminal behaviour in the eighteenth century. He is associated with a school of thought known as 'Classicism'. He argued that criminal behaviour could be understood as a product of rational free will. In other words, he argued that criminals choose to commit crime by calculating the pleasure (eg obtaining stolen goods) and pain (eg getting caught and being punished) involved. Crime was thus a consequence of hedonistic reasoning as criminals prioritised the search for pleasure. Later in this text, we will explore how this school of thought has come to influence other explanations of crime and criminal justice policy in the 1980s and 1990s.

INDIVIDUAL POSITIVISM

Alternative explanations developed in the nineteenth century and suggested that crime could be explained in terms of biological factors (a belief that individuals are born criminal) or psychological factors (a belief that a criminal mind or personality exists). Collectively these explanations are known as **individual positivism**. Positivism refers to the belief that modern scientific methods can be applied to all social problems, including crime.

The key elements of individual positivistic approaches are as follows:

- Individual behaviour is determined.
- Crime is caused by individual abnormality.
- Criminals are pathological and distinct from non-criminals.

Lombroso (1876) conducted one of the earliest studies in this tradition. He studied a group of male Italian criminals and argued that criminals were more likely to have certain physical characteristics which stem from their biological inferiority or defectiveness. He suggested that these features might include large jaws and cheekbones, extra fingers and toes and long arms. Based on this evidence, he argued that people were 'born criminal' and that criminals resemble more primitive human beings. He also studied female offenders. In this later work, he suggested that:

A comparison of the criminal skull with the skulls of normal women reveals the fact that female criminals approximate more to male, both criminal and non-criminal, than to normal women to males, both criminal and non-criminal, than to normal women.

Lombroso and Ferrero, 1895, p 28

Study point

Study the quotation above which is taken from Lombroso and Ferrero's work *The Female Offender*. They suggest that women who commit crime are different from women who do not. Do you agree with this view? Do you think criminal behaviour can be explained in terms of biology?

Sociologists have been highly critical of these early approaches because they identify crime as a social rather than an individual problem. The functionalist tradition retained the commitment to positivism but suggested that crime was caused by social rather than individual pathology. The task for sociology was to scientifically study the causes of crime and to locate them in social, economic and political conditions. While the development of sociological approaches has radically altered the criminological agenda, some researchers still adhere to the view that crime can be explained in terms of individual factors. For example, **Mednick** et al (1987) focus on genetic explanations and argue that some factor is transmitted by convicted parents. Moreover, the notion that criminals are pathological in some way is commonly used as a popular explanation of crime.

Activity

Make a list of all of the reasons why sociologists must reject biological and psychological theories of the origins of criminal behaviour.

FUNCTIONALIST APPROACHES

Durkheim (1895) wrote one of the earliest sociological works on crime. His work has contributed greatly to the development of functionalism and will be discussed again in Chapter 7 when we consider the act of suicide. A sociologist who adopts a functionalist perspective investigates how the parts, structures or systems of society are interrelated. Functionalists suggest that society functions in a similar way to the human body, with all parts playing a function in maintaining a healthy organism. This idea is known as the **organic analogy**. For functionalists, harmony and consensus are viewed as the norm in a healthy society. From this perspective, crime can be viewed as dysfunctional because it seems to threaten the stability of society. The presence of crime suggests that social problems exist and consequently functionalists looked to society for explanations of crime. Crime, they suggested, could best be explained in terms of social, rather than individual, pathology.

DURKHEIM

Crime as normal, inevitable and functional

Durkheim challenged some of these ideas and questioned whether crime was dysfunctional. Durkheim noted that crime was a feature of all societies and suggested it must, therefore, have a positive function. He argued that crime and punishment maintain social solidarity through establishing moral boundaries and strengthening the collective conscience; the beliefs and values shared by a community. Pathological acts such as crime are always defined in contrast to normality. Responding to crime helps to emphasise conformity and moral standards because crime brings people together in condemning the deviant. Traditionally, this was achieved through the involvement of the community in the public punishment of criminals. Today, the media has an important role to play in this respect. It presents horrific crimes and unites people in expressing their outrage at these acts and those committing them.

For Durkheim, a crime-free society could never be achieved. Without crime, he felt societies would be extremely repressive and incapable of adapting to social change. For example, he suggests that some modern societies would not have freedom of thought without individuals violating the regulations that historically prevented it. Whilst he did not think crime was desirable, he emphasised its positive functions.

Study point
Eco-warriors and environmental activists may break the law, but are they also good for society?

However, Durkheim did concede that certain rates of crime could be dysfunctional and could lead to social disintegration.

Points of evaluation

The work of Durkheim has been influential but his arguments can be questioned. **Downes** and **Rock** (1998) draw our attention to a number of issues:

- We are in danger of neglecting the negative effects of crime on individuals, families and communities if we view crime as functional for society.
- Who is crime functional for? The community responses to crime that Durkheim explores may be whipped up to support the interests of the powerful.
- At what point does crime become pathological rather than normal? At what point does crime destroy rather than integrate communities? These issues are left unexplored in Durkheim's work.

MERTON AND STRAIN THEORY

Many of the ideas first formulated by Durkheim have been applied by other sociologists. The concept of **anomie**, which Durkheim developed from his study of suicide (see Chapter 7), has been used to explain the causes of crime. Durkheim defines anomie as 'normlessness'. He noted that society encourages individualism and unlimited aspirations, but that these cannot always be realistically achieved. Unless society imposed new regulations on aspirations, a social state of anomie would occur, resulting in personal crises.

Merton (1938) used the concept of anomie and suggested that in society, socially produced aspirations often exceed what is obtainable through legitimate opportunities. Crime results as one possible response when there is a divergence between cultural goals and institutionalised means. Cultural goals refer to the goals through which success and status in society are defined.

Merton was studying US society in the 1930s and the cultural goal here was the 'American Dream'. This refers to the ideal of open and infinite opportunity for all and involved an emphasis on material wealth. Merton noted how the 'American Dream' did not fit easily with US society which was divided by social class and ethnicity. For some groups, opportunities were blocked. Thus they found themselves in a society with aspirations of material wealth (eg owning a car) and the inability to obtain material wealth through conventional means (eg working hard to earn enough money to pay for the car).

Merton identifies five responses to this 'strain' in the social structure of society. Applied to the example above, these responses are to:

1 Continue to work hard to earn enough money to pay for the car, even if this is unrealistic (conformity).

2 Obtain the car by other means such as theft (innovation).
3 Abandon the desire to own a car, but to continue to work hard (ritualism).
4 Become a deviant by establishing different cultural goals and different ways to achieve them (retreatism).
5 Challenge the status quo by attempting to introduce new cultural goals and ways to achieve them (rebellion).

In sum, Merton argues that the nature of US society creates crime. Criminality occurs particularly when individuals are unable to obtain the cultural goals of society through legitimate means and turn to illegitimate ones.

Points of evaluation

Merton's work has been highly influential and has impacted greatly on the work of sub-cultural theorists discussed later in this chapter. However, we might ask the following questions about his work:

1 Do all societies have shared cultural goals?
2 If so, are the goals the same for everyone, or are they different for different social groups eg women and men?
3 How successfully can Merton's ideas be used to explain crime that is not for material gain, such as vandalism?
4 Does Merton's theory enable us to explain crime such as white-collar crime?

Study point
Evaluate the suggestion that Merton's theorising does not fit the situation in Britain where class structures and class consciousness mean that few people have ever aspired to long-range social mobility or wealth acquisition.

THE CHICAGO SCHOOL

In the 1920s and 1930s, sociologists at the University of Chicago embarked on a systematic study of all aspects of their local urban environment. This work was positivist in orientation and mapped the distribution of crime in the city of Chicago. From their empirical studies, they argued that social disorganisation was the cause of crime. The highest rates of crime were found in the inner city which was an area characterised by poor housing, poverty, ethnic and cultural diversity and little sense of community. Thus they argued that it was the nature of neighbourhoods, not the nature of the individuals who lived there, which determined the level of criminality. This work is discussed in more detail in Chapter 4.

Is the environment or the population to blame for high levels of crime?

Later work by members of the Chicago School demonstrated a shift away from positivistic approaches, although it was heavily influenced by functionalism. Instead, sociologists used detailed case studies, applying qualitative and observational techniques to examine the perspective and attitudes of criminals. This work involved immersion in the social world of groups involved in criminal or deviant activities. Examples include:

- Thrasher, F. (1927) *The Gang*
- Shaw, C. (1930) *The Jack Roller: A Delinquent Boy's Own Story*
- Whyte, W. (1943) *Street Corner Society*.

The work of the Chicago sociologists highlighted the normality of criminal or other deviant activities within particular social groups, usually made up of lower-class males. Their research interest was focused on groups not individuals and these researchers emphasised socialisation and the learning of delinquent values as the causes of criminal behaviour. The existence of these groups, they argued, could be explained in terms of social factors such as unemployment and lack of social acceptance. Each group generates a distinct set of values which determined status and acceptance within the group. This tradition of work led to the development of sub-cultural approaches by researchers working in the USA and Britain. We will now critically review key US studies which adopt a sub-cultural approach.

Activity
What ethical and practical difficulties would a sociologist experience in trying to penetrate and observe a gang whose main shared activities are based on petty crime?

SUB-CULTURAL APPROACHES

Cohen (1955) was the first sociologist to systematically use the concept of culture and sub-culture to explain delinquency (Heidensohn 1989). Delinquency was the language used at the time to refer to the criminal and deviant acts of young people. Cohen noted that young people often committed delinquent acts in groups or gangs and suggested that these groups could be described as delinquent sub-cultures. We can define delinquent sub-culture as:

Social groups characterised by a commitment to values which are considered, within the dominant value system, to be criminal or antisocial.

Collins Dictionary of Sociology quoted in *Sociology Review*, April 1993

Cohen disagreed with Merton's view that delinquency was always directed towards achieving goals. He pointed out that some delinquent acts such as vandalism or violence were 'non-utilitarian and malicious and negativistic' (1955). Cohen suggested that the young people he studied were subjected to a series of middle-class goals which they felt required to measure their lives against. Rather than using innovative measures to achieve these goals as Merton suggests, Cohen argued that the reaction of lower-class youth was to create an oppositional value system, thus rejecting middle-class values. For Cohen, the growth of delinquent sub-cultures helped to counter young people's sense of failure and status frustration by providing a different source of status.

In later work, Cohen (Cohen and Short 1958) refined his ideas about delinquent sub-cultures and suggested that there were three kinds of sub-cultural response to dominant values:

1   the violent conflict sub-culture
2   the drug sub-culture
3   the semi-professional thief sub-culture.

This has many parallels with the typology offered by **Cloward** and **Ohlin** (1960). They were influenced by Merton's work but felt two issues were unexplored. The first was the process by which anomie leads to crime. The second was the reasons why an individual may choose one response rather than another, for example innovation rather than rebellion.

Using the concept of 'differential association' which emphasises that those exposed to more criminal than non-criminal values are more likely to adopt criminal values (Sutherland 1947), they suggested that young people will be exposed to different kinds of criminal values depending on their local area and culture. They identified three main categories of delinquent sub-culture:

1 Conflict sub-cultures found in areas with a history and tradition of violence and conflict between gangs.
2 Criminal sub-cultures found in areas with a pre-existing criminal culture which juvenile delinquents could become part of.
3 Retreatist sub-cultures consisting of 'drop outs' such as drug users, vagrants and alcoholics.

For Cloward and Ohlin (1961), the type of delinquent response was largely dependent on the illegitimate opportunities available.

Points of evaluation

Although highly influential in terms of the development of the sociology of crime and deviance, there has been a great deal of critical discussion of these approaches. Critical commentaries have focused on the following issues:

1 *Do delinquent sub-cultures really exist?*
   Other authors have suggested that most delinquency is committed by individuals or pairs of individuals rather than gangs (Kitsuse and Dietrick 1959). It has also been suggested that, whilst gangs did exist, they were far from widespread and their members lacked a total commitment to delinquent values (Yablonsky 1962).
2 *Do delinquent groups hold values that are opposed to mainstream culture?*
   Miller (1958) suggests that delinquent values such as toughness, masculinity and a tolerance of many forms of theft were part of conventional lower-class culture. Miller challenged the view that separate sub-cultures with values opposed to mainstream culture existed. **Sykes** and **Matza** (1957) also suggest that delinquent values were not necessarily oppositional. They noted that delinquents regularly used ' techniques of neutralisation' to account for their actions and these echo conventional values. These 'techniques' include denying any harm was done or denying responsibility for their actions.
3 *How do sub-cultural approaches explain conformity amongst many lower-class males?*
   Sub-cultural theories tend to over-predict delinquency. Whilst many theories recognised that not all lower-class youth became delinquents, many could not explain why the majority did engage in delinquency (Downes and Rock 1998). Moreover, they did not really deal with the issue that young people often drift between conformity and deviance (Matza 1964).

4   *Are there any middle-class sub-cultures?*
Sub-cultural approaches have focused only on lower-class youth and thus contribute to the belief that only lower-class youth are delinquent. **Kitsuse** and **Dietrick** (1959), in their critique of Cohen's work, suggest that middle-class gang delinquency was under-reported.
5   *Where are the women in these sociological studies?*
Studies have tended to only focus on males. Women were not seen to be members of gangs and rarely got a mention, even as the girlfriends of male gang members. Cohen (1955) distinguished between boys' and girls' delinquency. Cloward and Ohlin (1960) offer some discussion of masculinity. However, the terms 'gender' and 'masculinity' were misunderstood (Heidensohn 1989). More recently, a study has been conducted on female involvement in gangs (Campbell 1984) in New York. This documents how women are involved to a lesser extent than men, but they should not be treated as invisible.

The studies discussed in this chapter relate to fieldwork conducted in the USA. Britain has less of an established tradition of violent or criminal gangs. The work of Miller on working-class culture has had a greater influence on British work (Croall 1998). Work in Britain has emphasised youth culture and style rather than delinquent sub-cultures. Much of this research has been conducted by researchers within the Centre of Contemporary Cultural Studies at the University of Birmingham and offers a more radical view than earlier US work. Marxism influenced it more than functionalism. This work is discussed in more detail in the next chapter. Essentially it was concerned with issues of power and the State in capitalist society. Popular culture and deviant sub-cultures were analysed within this framework.

Activity
Summarise the criticisms that have been made of the sub-cultural approach to criminology.

EARLY MARXIST APPROACHES

Marxism, as we have just noted, has influenced sociologists searching for the causes of crime. Marx himself wrote little on crime specifically, but his theoretical framework can be applied to the study of crime. One of the key elements of Marxism is that all social phenomena (including crime) can be explained in terms of each society's economic relations. In a capitalist society, the private ownership of the means of production by the bourgeoisie creates structural inequality and conflict. In such societies, the bourgeoisie exploits the proletariat and thus crime can be seen as part of a struggle in which the economically powerless proletariat attempts to cope with the exploitation and poverty imposed on them.

Study point
Crime is considered to be a response to deprivation, alienation and lack of power, and, according to Marxist feminist thought, women are the most oppressed people in society. Does Marxism fully account for the fact that the females appear to commit less crime than males?

THE WORK OF BONGER

Bonger (1916), a Dutch academic, was the first to apply Marxist ideas to the study of crime. He made the following observations:

- Capitalism encourages egoistic tendencies and greed, thus encouraging criminal behaviour.
- Inequality in capitalist societies creates poverty amongst the proletariat, which causes crime.
- Criminal law exists to protect the interests of the bourgeoisie.

Bonger also noted how crime was not committed solely by the proletariat, but that crimes could also be committed by the bourgeoisie. He suggested that their powerful position gave them opportunities to commit crimes in a society which Bonger viewed as immoral. The theme of crimes of the bourgeoisie was developed further in the work of Sutherland in his pioneering study of white-collar crime.

Sutherland cannot be identified as a Marxist but his work has been influential in the sense that it put the issue of white-collar crime on the criminological agenda.

SUMMARY

In this chapter we have documented the early development of sociological explanations of crime and deviance. There was a shift from the sociological positivistic approach, focusing only on the social structure as a cause of crime, towards a more interpretative approach, which showed greater concern with human action. There was also the early beginnings of a more radical understanding of crime which included a concern with issues of power, the economy and the State. Increasingly, sociologists were beginning to put new areas of study on the criminological agenda such as crimes of the powerful.

Key Concept Activity

Look at the following terms. Explain what they mean in terms that you will remember. You may need to use a sociological dictionary:

- functionalism
- white-collar crime
- sub-culture
- the American dream
- anomie (functionalist)
- alienation (Marxist).

Group Work

Attempt to identify whether there is such a phenomenon as a sub-culture with different attitudes to crime compared to the general population. Collect together a bank of short statements that could be used to test social attitudes towards crime or unruly behaviour. Two possible statements are as follows:

1 It does not matter if you damage a car and then walk away. It was probably insured anyway.
2 Shoplifting from big supermarkets does not matter because the owners are so rich.

Everyone in the group should collect data from as wide a range and number of respondents as possible, noting social class, ages and gender. Ask people to denote agreement or disagreement with the statements. Pool your results. Are there actually very significant differences in attitudes between groups of people depending upon their age group, gender, social class or ethnicity? If you find that there are not, then perhaps you can call into question the notion of sub-culture. If there are significant differences, then perhaps you should consider why they might exist.

Coursework

'Attitudes to Rule-Breaking'

With the cooperation of your school or institution, identify a particular group of pupils who seem to be unwilling to accept the rules of the institution with regard to uniform or behaviour. Design an interview schedule and attempt to discover what members of the focus group feel about the school, something of their behaviour out of school and why it is important to them to break the rules that they do. Does their behaviour represent a genuine rejection of the moral values in your view?

Revision Hints

Be aware that each type of theory accounting for crime and deviance may adopt a different definition of the nature and origins of crime and may use different beliefs about the nature of humans as social animals. You can develop this type of thinking by extending the summary tables at the start of this chapter and the other chapters of this text.

You are also advised to start making notes on the various writers mentioned and to summarise their findings in a simple and manageable form. These notes are to provide you with supporting evidence for analytical and evaluative answers. Remember that the notes should be very brief *aide-memories* – answers that simply repeat lists of findings or offer detailed descriptions of what the researchers actually did will be penalised as description. The emphasis of your work must be analysis and evaluation. If you wish use the grid below as a guide for your notes.

Name of researcher	
Title and date of research	
Main perspective 50 words to summarise findings	

Exam Hints

This chapter is a popular examination topic and you should be sure that you fully understand the points covered. You may need to criticise the notion of structures in society that give rise to crime, or to comment on one or all of the theories in the light of other factors.

Two sample essay titles are offered below. The questions discussed are 'catch-all' in that the phrases which are underlined can be substituted with any number of alternatives to make entirely new questions. For example, in question one 'the middle classes' could replace the word 'women'.

1 *Evaluate the suggestion that traditional sociological perspectives have always tended to overlook the role of* <u>women</u> *in their analysis of criminal behaviour.*
   You would need to carefully consider the question and to identify what is meant by the 'role of women'. Are you to consider the question of women as victims or as perpetrators of crimes? Look at the theories that are considered

in the chapter and ask yourself why they fail to note the significance of females. Your conclusion may have to suggest it is because the thinking on offer is masculine and operates on a number of untested assumptions about who actually commits crime. You may wish to return to this question again after considering the next chapter of this text and at the end of the whole book.

2 *Assess the usefulness of sub-cultural theory to a sociological understanding of the causes of crime in our society.*

Any of the sociological theories mentioned in the chapter could replace the term 'sub-cultural theory'. Make sure that you have constructed a table containing both the strengths and weaknesses of each approach in advance of the examination.

You will certainly need to show awareness that sociological debate is not just between perspectives, but often within them as well. For example, sub-cultural theories are often described as being a development of functionalism despite the fact that the observational methodologies used are more frequently seen as typical of interactionism and, in Britain, sub-cultural work has been influenced by Marxism.

6

EXPLAINING CRIME AND DEVIANCE: THE GROWTH OF RADICAL APPROACHES

Introduction

THIS CHAPTER WILL explore the growth of radical approaches to explaining criminal and deviant behaviour. Earlier sociological explanations focused largely on the ways society encouraged people to behave in criminal or deviant ways, and sometimes suggested that such behaviours were determined by social forces outside the control of an individual. In contrast, interactionism which began to influence the sociology of crime and deviance in the 1960s began to explore the social reaction to criminal and deviant acts and gave priority to understanding the meanings individuals give to social actions.

The revival of Marxism in the 1970s inspired a number of explanations of crime including the 'new' criminology and critical criminology. This period also witnessed the development of feminist critiques which questioned the ability of many sociological perspectives to explain women's offending.

THINKING ABOUT REACTIONS TO CRIME

INTERACTIONIST APPROACHES

Interactionism originates from the work of **George Herbert Mead** (1934) and is concerned with understanding the processes which underpin social life and the mechanisms by which meanings are assigned to these processes. This perspective has been particularly influential in the USA.

Table 10: *Theorists, concepts and issues in this chapter*			
	KEY THEORISTS	KEY CONCEPTS	KEY IDEAS
Interactionism	Becker Lemert Cohen	Primary and secondary deviation Social reaction Deviant careers Deviancy amplification	Individuals become deviant though social processes. Societal reactions to deviance have implications for those labelled deviant and society.
Marxism	Chambliss Quinney Pearce	Capitalism Class conflict Inequality Political economy	Capitalism creates crime. Responses to crime reflect the interests of the bourgeoisie.
'New criminology'	Taylor, Walton and Young	Fully social theory of deviance Political economy Social psychology Social reaction	Sociologists need to develop a fully social theory of deviance and radical politics. Fundamental social change is needed to solve the problem of crime.
Critical criminology	Hall et al Scraton, Chadwick and Little	Class, gender, race (structured inequalities) Process of criminalisation (State)	The process of criminalisation is not simply a matter of controlling criminality, but of containing political opposition and perpetuating structured inequalities.
Feminist perspectives in criminology	Heidensohn Smart Carlen Gelshtorpe and Morris	Gender Patriarchy Economic marginalisation Social control Masculinity	Women have been neglected or misrepresented in theories of crime and criminal justice policies. Gender is an important category of analysis.

As a theoretical perspective, interactionism highlights the creative capacities of human actors and their ability to share understandings with each other. Those adopting an interactionist approach study interactions between people, how they are understood and how they are modified, refined and developed. One of the best-known theorists associated with this tradition is **Becker**. His work *Outsiders* (1963) was most frequently named in a survey of British criminologists (Rock 1994) as the publication which had the most influence on them.

Study point

At the time of writing, analysis of Becker's work is sadly under-represented on the Internet, though this may change as more British University sites come into operation. He is, however, well discussed in most textbooks and you are advised to ensure that your notes on this most influential of writers are comprehensive.

Becker and 'Outsiders'

Becker placed great emphasis on the social processes involved in becoming deviant. He studied marijuana (cannabis) users in California. His ethnographic study of the drug users was the basis for the development of **labelling theory**. Becker's work has two central themes running through it:

1 The process by which a particular behaviour is labelled deviant.

2 The impact of the labelling process on those labelled deviant.

Becker's central argument was succinctly summarised in the extract below from *Outsiders*.

> Social groups create deviance by making the rules whose infraction constitutes deviance and by applying the rules to other people and labelling them as outsiders. From this point of view, deviance is not a quality of the act the person commits, but rather a consequence of the application by others of rules and sanctions to an 'offender'. The deviant is one to whom the label has successfully been applied; deviant behaviour is behaviour that people so label.
>
> Becker, 1963, p 8–9

Becker's work was heavily influenced by the ideas of **Edwin Lemert**, who made a distinction between **primary** and **secondary deviance**. Lemert's definitions were:

- *Primary deviance* – the initial act.
- *Secondary deviance* – the deviance that takes place after a deviant label has been applied.

He suggested that being labelled 'deviant' might have a profound effect on an individual's subsequent behaviour. Becker applied these concepts to his study of marijuana users.

In his study, Becker did not explore in detail the reasons for the initial drug use. Indeed, this was a later criticism of his work, in that the origins of the first deviant behaviours remain unexplored. Rather he focused on the process of becoming a marijuana user and the consequence of being labelled deviant by society.

Drug use in the USA at the time of Becker's study was strictly forbidden and controlled by severe penalties. Consequently, the drug users he studied were labelled deviant by the rule enforcers and rule-makers whom Becker terms 'moral entrepreneurs'. Being labelled deviant leads to stigmatisation; people avoid the 'deviants' or behave differently towards them. The 'deviants' become excluded from normal activities and become outsiders. Thus, those labelled have to cope with a new identity. They may pursue a deviant 'career' by changing their lifestyle in a way that confirms their deviant status; for example, experimenting with new forms of drugs, becoming part of a drug subculture or 'dropping out' of society.

Activity

Organise a class discussion and consider the following questions:

1   What problems might you experience if you were to try to repeat Becker's study in contemporary Britain?
2   What problems would you experience if the deviant behaviour that you were attempting to study was even more unacceptable than drug-taking is in our culture?

The impact of the application of labels for the individual labelled and for society is explored by other interactionist sociologists who developed and applied the concept of deviancy amplification.

The amplification of deviant behaviour

Wilkins (1965) developed the concept of **deviancy amplification**. His argument is that under certain conditions, society will define as deviant a group of people who depart from valued norms in some way. The negative social reaction may lead to exclusion of those individuals from mainstream society and thus increase the possibility that the group will act even more deviantly. If it does, societal reaction will increase at the same pace and greater deviancy will be induced, producing further reactions. A deviancy amplification spiral is created where each increase in social control is matched by a corresponding increase in deviancy among the groups that have identified themselves as deviant. This can be best illustrated as a diagram (see below).

Deviant actions	Societal actions
	10 Deviant group rejected and experiences massive social hostility until public interest moves towards another area of concern.
9 Deviant group becomes increasingly marginalised and no longer feels bound by the normal rules of society. The group are then free to commit more outrageous acts.	
	8 Public comment is increasingly critical and deviant behaviour becomes 'problematised'. Laws may even be changed to penalise act more severely.
7 Deviant group feels rejected, misunderstood and outlawed by society.	
	6 Increased public criticism.
5 Self-defined deviant groups begin to form	
	4 Increasing policing. Strict penalties imposed.
3 Act seems attractive and dangerous to individuals who then engage in it.	
	2 Defined as deviant by police and/or media coverage.
1 Initial act.	

Study point

How well do you feel that the above process could be applied to any particular form of crime common among young people such as 'joy-riding' or ecstasy use? Could you apply the above analysis to public reaction to paedophiles?

Cohen applied this concept to the study of Mods and Rockers in Britain in the 1960s. He emphasised the role of the media in amplifying the activities of youth groups labelled as deviant.

Cohen: Folk Devil and Moral Panics

Stan Cohen's (1973) research explored the social reaction to the Mods and Rockers disturbances of 1964 through the mid 1960s. His work is important because it developed the concept of a moral panic, which has been used to describe media and political reactions to particular events or groups of people. The typical pattern of a moral panic is that certain events trigger a sense of strong moral outrage. At their height, these reactions are characterised by exaggeration and distortion and then the whole story seems to lose news value and is no longer at the forefront of people's concern.

Mods and Rockers were names given to two working-class teenage gangs who gathered at the seaside resort of Clacton over an Easter bank holiday. Some scuffles between the two groups took place but there was little in the way of violence or vandalism. However, these events were reported in the media as a 'day of terror' with violence reigning between rival gangs. The consequences of this were three-fold (Muncie 1996).

1 Increased and heavy-handed police surveillance.
2 The differences between the two groups were exaggerated and young people were encouraged to identify with one or the other of the groups by media coverage. The imagery of conflict led to further clashes at other seaside resorts.
3 The continuing disturbances attracted more news coverage, increased police activity and furthered police concern. This eventually had an impact on the process of justice as magistrates were applauded for handing out extreme sentences for relatively minor offences.

Thus a deviancy amplification spiral was set in motion. Cohen suggested that this was part of a postwar moral panic about youth culture, with young people cast in the roles of 'folk devils'. Youth was seen as a problem.

Activity

Suggest a number of different events that have been covered in the media in recent years, which may have been sensationalised or over-reported.

Points of evaluation

Later in this chapter we will explore how the concept of deviancy amplification was used by those working in a critical criminological tradition with a more explicit focus on issues of power and the role of the State. First let us consider some of the strengths and weaknesses of interactionist approach.

Strengths

The interactionist approach has a number of strengths:

• It notes how deviance is a socially constructed concept and thus historically and culturally relative (see Chapter 2).
• It challenges the idea of a value consensus regarding what acts are defined as deviant.
• It rejects the idea that deviants are distinct from so-called 'normal' people and are pathological.
• It challenges the view that deviants are controlled by forces that drive them into deviance.

- It considers all social actors involved in the process of labelling acts as deviant and in creating deviant identities.
- It questions the role of the media and the impact of moral and political campaigns on crime and deviance in society.

Weaknesses

However, some important criticisms have been made of interactionist studies:

- **Gouldner** (1968) argues that they over-romanticise deviants and treat them as 'not-so-bad' after all. He believed that interactionists view deviants as victims who are not responsible for their actions.
- **Liazos** (1972) suggests that interactionists concentrate too much on 'exotic' forms of deviance. He dubs this tradition as the study of 'nuts, sluts and perverts'. The consequence of this focus is to gloss over the crimes of the powerful such as covert, institutional violence and to ignore 'run of the mill' crimes such as shoplifting which make up the majority of criminal offences.
- It does not explain the origins of deviant behaviour which may precede the labelling process.
- It glosses over the importance of structural factors such as social class and gender.
- Deviants may adopt a deviant identify without being given a label by others.

Activity
Ask teachers whom you know well, and who are open with you, about how they can recognise potentially 'difficult' children. What signals do they look for? How soon do they feel that they can tell that the child may be a problem for them?
Who initiates the process of labelling a child as difficult? Could it be the child, who engages in certain forms of key behaviour, that triggers the labelling process? Does the teacher actively set out to label children in your view? How significant is previous experience in enabling a teacher to make judgements?
What have you learned about the origins of deviant behaviour and subsequent labels from this exercise? Is the process a simple one or are a number of factors possibly involved?

THE REVIVAL OF MARXIST APPROACHES

Interactionist approaches opened up a concern with the process of criminalisation, but failed to explore this process in the context of the social, political and economic organisation of society. Whilst it paved the way for the politicisation of the sociological study of crime, interactionist approaches left a number of questions still to be explored. For instance, they did not ask why some acts were defined as criminal while others were not. This issue became a central theme of Marxist criminology, which developed an analysis of the political economy of crime. This form of analysis explores the political and economical context in which crime occurs and is responded to.

In the previous chapter, we noted how the ideas of Marx influenced the work of Bonger who was writing at the beginning of the twentieth century. However, this theoretical tradition had little impact on the sociology of crime and deviance until the 1970s. At that time, a growing number of sociologists offered Marxist-inspired analyses of the problem of crime. Particularly influential were the writings of **Chambliss** (1975), **Quinney** (1977) and **Pearce** (1976). These theorists shared the view that there was a relationship between the mode of economic production and the nature and extent of crime in society. For them the problem of crime varies from society to society depending on the political and economic structures.

KEY THEMES OF THE MARXIST APPROACH

Inequality and class conflict

Capitalist societies promote inequality and class conflict and therefore are criminogenic societies.

Criminal behaviour is … the inevitable expression of class conflict resulting from the inherently exploitative nature of economic relations.

Chambliss, 1975

For Marxists, high levels of crime in capitalist societies are unsurprising. Capitalism creates crime because it promotes and prioritises self-interest, personal gain and the accumulation of wealth and personal possessions. This takes place in a society characterised by the unequal distribution of resources and class conflict.

Bourgeois self-interest

Acts are defined as criminal because it is in the interests of the bourgeoisie to define them as criminal. As we noted in Chapter 2, Marxists argue that the criminal law is not neutral but instead is an instrument which predominantly benefits and secures the interests of the bourgeoisie. When certain kinds of behaviours are deemed 'criminal', this reflects the success of the bourgeoisie in criminalising acts that threaten the survival of the current state of society. A good example of this is the criminalisation of trade union activities such as picketing in the 1980s following the miners' strike.

Ideology and the operation of criminal justice

Marxists suggest that, not only does the criminal law reflect the interests of the powerful, so too does the criminal justice system. The criminal justice system rarely responds to crimes of the powerful such as white-collar crime or State crime and instead focuses on crimes of the powerless.

Solutions to crime

For Marxists, crime can only be dealt with through major social, economic and political change. The solution to the problem of crime is simple yet radical for Marxists. If capitalism creates crime, the only solution is the restructuring of society, socially, politically and economically to create a socialist society. For Marx, this could only be achieved through revolution.

Points of evaluation

Whilst Marxist theory advances our understanding of why only certain behaviours are criminalised by the State and explores how capitalist societies generate certain patterns of crime, a number of problems remain with Marxist explanations:

- Marxist views tend to represent working-class crime as a creative response to oppression but the reality is that much working-class crime is directed at working-class people. Moreover, they do not fully explain why all working-class people do not commit crime.
- Marxists have been accused of **reductionism**. This is the criticism that they reduce all problems to an explanation in terms of economic relations.
- **Determinism** is the idea that events, actions and beliefs are determined by a prior structure. Effectively people are seen as unable to choose their own actions because they merely respond to external stimuli. Marxists tend to view the behaviour of individuals as largely governed by external forces. Thus their accounts are often described as deterministic. Some theorists would suggest that individuals (oppressed or otherwise) retain some autonomy or free will which enables them to decide whether to carry out criminal or deviant actions.
- Feminists would ask why female crime is relatively uncommon if the most exploited people in society are the most likely to commit crime. Marxist feminists would argue that women are doubly exploited by capitalism and patriarchy (the dominance of men over women).
- We can question their belief that communist societies are crime-free by researching levels of crime in the former Soviet Union and other countries of Eastern Europe. However, many Marxists would counter this because they would not consider these societies either socialist or communist.

Activity
There are a number of Web sites relating to Marxism. Many are highly theoretical and others are very political and demand a wide knowledge of Marxism. They do however, give a good flavour of the debate. You will probably find some interesting information if you key in 'Marx' and 'sociology'. At the time of writing, a good Australian site can be found at the following address: http://www.anu.edu.au/polsci/marx/marx.html Other sociology sites are listed at the end of the book.

THE 'NEW' CRIMINOLOGY

Taylor, **Walton** and **Young** (1973) tried to overcome some of these problems in their highly influential text: *The New Criminology*. These theorists attempted to combine Marxist principles with insights gained from interactionist approaches. In other words, they aimed to bring together a concern with structural factors, particularly political economy, class relations and State practices (Marxism) with a concern with social reaction, individual meaning and action (interactionism). Using this framework, they aimed to provide a 'fully social theory of deviance'. Taylor, Walton and Young argued that explanations of crime need to consider the seven different elements discussed below:

1 *The wider origins of the deviant act (political economy of crime)*
    Taylor, Walton and Young argue that a criminal (or a deviant) act must be examined in the wider social, political and economic context in which it occurs. This is clearly influenced by Marxism.

2 *Immediate origins of the deviant act (social psychology of crime)*
    However, individuals do not simply respond to structural factors (eg social class) and individuals will respond to these factors in different ways. Taylor, Walton and Young tried to avoid the determinism which characterises Marxist explanations through exploring how human actors make choices, even if they are influenced by structural factors. For example, not all people who experience poverty commit crime, but their choices about whether to offend or not are likely to be heavily influenced by their position in society.

3 *The actual act (social dynamics)*
    Choosing a criminal or deviant solution does not necessarily lead to crime being committed. Individuals may be unable to carry out their criminal or deviant plans. As Taylor, Walton and Young (1973, p 271) note:

> *A working-class adolescent … may want to engage in hedonistic activities (eg finding immediate pleasure through the use of alcohol, drugs, or in extensive sexual activities) or he may choose to kick back at a rejecting society (eg through acts of vandalism) … But he may find that these options themselves are not easily achieved.*

Consequently, sociologists need to explore the social dynamics surrounding actual acts.

4　*Immediate origins of social reaction (social psychology of social reaction)*
Taking insights from labelling theory, Taylor, Walton and Young note the need to consider the reactions of others to the behaviour of an individual. This involves considering the reactions of the witnesses to particular behaviours, and a wider audience including the criminal justice system and people significant to the 'offender'. They emphasise that people make choices about how to respond to events and we need to consider the factors that influence their choices.

5　*Wider origins of deviant reaction (political economy of social reaction)*
Choices are influenced by structural factors. The State has an important role to play in influencing the reaction of criminal justice professionals. It also influences the public response because it periodically defines particular types of behaviour, or particular groups of individuals, as a problem for society. Later in this chapter we explore this theme in the work of **Hall** et al who consider responses to 'mugging' in the 1970s.

6　*The outcome of the social reaction on deviant's further action*
The sixth concern of Taylor, Walton and Young is with the relationship between the social reaction to the deviant and/or criminal behaviour and the impact of that social reaction. In other words, they argue that sociologists need to explore whether or not there is an impact on their future criminal and/or deviant careers. The influence of labelling theorists is very considerable here.

7　*The nature of the deviant process as a whole*
Taylor, Walton and Young argue that not only do all these elements need to be considered, but sociologists also need to think about the relationship between the different elements.

The aim of their work was not only to outline a framework for explaining crime and deviance, but also to promote radical solutions to the problem of crime. For Taylor, Walton and Young, this involved the abolition of inequalities of wealth and power and tolerance of human diversity.

Activity
Summarise the above seven elements of the 'new' criminological perspective in your own words. Evaluate the theory by considering how useful or practical the issues raised are for criminologists who are: • attempting to explain crime • attempting to design research projects • interested in finding solutions to the problem of crime.

CRITICAL CRIMINOLOGICAL APPROACHES

By the mid 1970s, the sociology of crime and deviance was highly politicised. The growing concern with the process of criminalisation provided the backdrop for critical criminologists to explore the ways in which power associated with the capitalist State asserts itself in relation to crime. They took their inspiration from a number of theorists including **Foucault**, **Gramsci** and **Marx**.

In simple terms, critical criminology seeks to explore the ways in which the variables of class, ethnicity and gender are played out in relation to crime and criminal justice. Their concern is not just with discriminatory practices but the ways in which these structured inequalities are perpetuated. For example, such theorists note how State practices serve to marginalise and consequently criminalise some groups and not others. Marxists had highlighted the criminalisation of the proletariat. Critical criminologists extended this analysis to ethnic minorities and women.

'MUGGING' AND THE RACIALISATION OF STREET CRIME

Hall et al (1978) analysed concerns about 'mugging' in Britain in 1972. They argued that 'mugging' was an historical convention (see Chapter 2), a label attached to an existing street crime rather than a new crime. Bringing together these crimes under the new label of 'mugging', the State was able to mobilise popular anxieties and create a 'law and order' society. Fear of crime was used by the State to divert public attention away from economic and political crises and define problems in Britain in terms of lawlessness rather than inequality or social deprivation. To use Cohen's term, there was a moral panic about 'mugging', with black youth identified as the folk devils.

Activity

Assess whether ethnicity is still a component of the social construction of a 'mugger' by asking people to describe the 'typical characteristics' of a mugger. How many respondents of your small survey mention ethnicity, even indirectly? Remember however, that in the 1970s there was very little social stigma attached to expressing overtly hostile and racist views, whereas in today's society many people are a little more cautious when considering issues of ethnicity.

THE CRIMINALISATION OF WOMEN

Chadwick and **Little** (1987) combine critical criminological concerns with a feminist perspective to explore how the State acts to women who move out of, or threaten traditionally conceived boundaries of femininity. This reinforces gender roles in advanced capitalist societies and perpetuates inequality. Examples of the criminalisation of women include:

- prostitutes
- women at Greenham Common who led an anti-nuclear weapon campaign
- single mothers.

Scraton and **Chadwick** (1991) argue that an analysis of issues of class, race and gender is central to studying the problem of crime and the process of criminalisation. This wider concern with issues of race and gender departs greatly from traditional perspectives, which tend to focus predominantly on class. This can largely be attributed to the influence of feminist criminologists.

Activity

Collect cuttings from newspapers which relate to male and female offenders. Analyse this material by asking the following questions:

1   What images are presented of criminal women?
2   Are the images presented of criminal women very different from those of criminal men?
3   Are public reactions different towards female and male offenders?

Points of evaluation

The 'new' and critical criminological perspectives suggested new ways of thinking about crime and deviance. Their radical views have attracted a great deal of criticism. Consider the following issues:

1 Is it possible to combine a concern with structural factors (Marxism) and a concern with action (interactionism)?

2 Do the 'new' and critical criminological perspectives avoid the trap of economic determinism; a criticism often levelled at Marxist-inspired theories?

3 Are these perspectives too idealistic in that they emphasise structural change as the only way of dealing with the problem of crime?

Those who adopt a realist approach to crime have levelled the criticism of idealism against the critical and 'new' criminologies. They criticise these perspectives for failing to offer policy suggestions that might provide practical help to those who experience the effects of crime. We return to the development of realist approaches in Chapters 8 and 9. You need to be aware that realist approaches have been developed by those on the political left (as we discussed in Chapter 3) and the right. Whilst they have features in common, they have differing views of both the causes of crime and ways of preventing it. Those who adopt a feminist perspective also share their concern with the effects of crime.

FEMINIST PERSPECTIVES IN CRIMINOLOGY

Students of sociology soon become aware of the variety of competing perspectives that characterise the discipline. They should also be aware that there is considerable debate within each tradition. This also applies to feminism. Feminists have been influenced by all the dominant theoretical traditions (see Tong 1998). You should also be aware that the three main feminist traditions are **liberal feminism**, **Marxist or socialist feminism** and **radical feminism**. Each brings its own concerns to the debate.

We discussed earlier the work of Chadwick and Little which combined insights from socialist feminism and critical criminology. Despite these ongoing debates, some common ground can be seen with feminist perspectives within criminology. **Gelsthorpe** and **Morris** (1990) define a feminist perspective as:

- accepting the view that women experience subordination on the basis of their sex
- seeking to work towards the elimination of social subordination.

FEMINIST CRITIQUES

Female Offenders

The second wave of the women's movement in the late 1960s and early 1970s introduced a new dimension to criminological debates. It began by developing a critique of the different explanations of women's involvement in crime. Early influential works included Heidensohn (1968), **Klein** (1973) and **Smart** (1976).

Feminist critiques noted that women who offend are usually treated in one of the following two ways:

1 **Neglected**: women were absent from theories of crime which were usually developed from studies of men and offered as general theories of crime.
2 **Misrepresented**: if women were included they were usually portrayed in stereotypical ways, usually as pathological and mad rather than bad.

Women have also been neglected in terms of penal policy. For example, women prisoners have often not been considered in key policy documents and official reports. Consequently, feminists (particularly liberal feminists) focused their efforts on the topic of women and crime in order to remedy this situation. There are also examples of misrepresentation. Women who offend are often seen as pathological, thus they are more likely to receive a psychiatric disposal (Allen 1987) and one of the largest women's prisons, Holloway (London), was built to resemble a psychiatric hospital rather than a prison (Rock 1996).

Women as Victims

An important contribution of radical feminists has been to expose women's experiences of victimisation. They have exposed the fact that women are victims of hidden crime, including domestic and sexual violence. They have exposed the extent of hidden crime against women through sensitive use of the survey method (see Chapter 3) but have also conducted qualitative research with victims. Their work has involved asking new questions such as, 'why are women unable to leave men who batter them?' The traditional approaches might tackle the same question but ask instead, 'why do they stay?' There is an important qualitative difference between the two questions. The second contains an accusatory challenge and fails to realise the barriers women face when deciding to leave violent men.

Therefore, an important dimension to their work has been to challenge stereotypes and myths: principally that women are in some way to blame for the victimisation they experience. These myths impact on the way women are treated by the criminal justice system and feminists working in this area have been influential in campaigning for legal reforms and changes in the criminal justice response.

Activity
Consider any of the recent well-publicised cases involving females who have been accused or convicted of a very serious crime such as murder. Past examples might include: Myra Hindley, Rosemary West or Louise Woodward. To what extent is it possible to apply the above analyses to the media coverage, public and judicial responses to their cases?

EXPLAINING GENDERED PATTERNS OF OFFENDING

Explanations of women's offending have a long history dating back to the work of **Lombroso** and **Ferrero**. Early explanations tend to focus on women's biology or psychology as an explanation for their crimes. These have been strongly criticised and more recent explanations consider social factors. Other explanations are discussed in the following section:

Liberation

Adler (1975) and **Simon** (1975) suggested that rising crime rates amongst women in the USA could be explained by women's changing position in society. They argue that as women in the Western world became increasingly emancipated and were able to behave more like men in different areas of social life, they would be increasingly involved in crime, particularly unfeminine forms of crime such as violence. As opportunities for women increased, so too would criminal opportunities.

Marginalisation

The liberation thesis has been heavily criticised by **Carlen** (1988). Her starting point is that women are much more likely to commit property crime than violent crime and this can be explained in terms of their economic marginalisation. Based on interviews with female offenders, Carlen (1988) argues that women's law-breaking is a survival strategy, a rational and coherent response to their awareness of the social disabilities imposed on them by discriminatory and exploitative gender relations. However, Carlen is keen to avoid deterministic accounts and argues that we also need to consider why female crime rates are so low. This can be explained in terms of the gendered nature of social control.

Social control

Other theorists (Heidensohn 1996, Morris 1987, Smart 1976) have asked why women *do not* commit crime rather than why they *do*. Women are constrained by the roles they are expected to play in society. They have fewer resources and opportunities to commit crime and they are subject to a level of social control which inhibits their participation in crime (see Chapter 8). This helps us to understand the major gender differences in patterns of offending (see Chapter 4).

Masculinity

Criminologists have been paying increasing attention to masculinity (Newburn and Stanko 1994, Jefferson 1997). This work has added some important insights to criminological debates. It has demonstrated that masculinity is a cultural role which men adopt. It is something constructed in the struggles of everyday life, through interaction, and men learn to behave as men. Many writers talk about masculinities and emphasise the differences between men based on class, age, ethnic origin and sexual orientation. The characteristics of the dominant form of masculinity in society include aggression, physical action, toughness and the need to maintain power. These characteristics can be linked to different forms of criminal behaviour such as violence, white-collar crime and football hooliganism (see Newburn and Stanko 1994).

Activity

Identify the characteristics of the male heroes of recent action-movie cinema releases. How do they solve their problems? What moral values do they display? What relationships do they have with females?

How might a young male who followed these role models behave in his own life?

THE IMPACT OF FEMINIST PERSPECTIVES ON CRIMINOLOGY

Has feminism had any impact on criminology? Heidensohn (1995, p 5) suggests that:

What has been achieved is no earthquake, not even a tremor. But the landscape has altered, at least in the English-speaking world.

Writers in the feminist tradition have made a number of important achievements. These include the fact that they have:

1   exposed criminology as 'malestream' not mainstream
2   made women visible
3   challenged stereotypes
4   introduced new questions, new topics and new methods
5   illuminated sexism in theory, policy and practice
6   raised awareness of the importance of gender.

In 1990, Gelsthorpe and Morris suggested that feminist criminology is a project under construction. Important progress has been made since then. There has been a great deal of attention paid to the link between masculinities and crime. The process of gendering criminology is underway but appears far from complete. There is still much work to be done in exploring the relationship between gender and crime. Moreover, criminal justice policy still remains driven by the needs of male offenders with little consideration of its implications for women. This is vividly described in recent works on women's imprisonment (Carlen 1998, Devlin 1998).

SUMMARY

In a relatively short space of time, the sociology of crime and deviance changed dramatically. Interactionism emerged in the 1960s as an innovative way of thinking about crime. It acted as a source of inspiration for later perspectives by encouraging the development of more radical and political approaches when combined with the insights of Marxism. Critical and feminist criminology brought issues of race and gender to a discipline that had traditionally focused on social class. We return to theories of crime in Chapter 9 when we explore current trends in criminological theory. Internal debate and controversy now rack criminology. Criminologists are united only by their fascination with 'crime'. As we discussed in Chapter 2, there remains the problem that there is still no agreed definition of what crime actually is!

Activity
Re-read Chapters 5 and 6 carefully. Identify each sociological perspective and attempt a working definition of what actually constitutes a crime or criminal behaviour from that perspective. Which theoretical perspective do you find most satisfactory from your own point of view? Make sure that you give three reasons to support your evaluation.

STUDY GUIDES

Key Concept Activity

You should read this chapter thoroughly and on a regular basis until you understand the points that are being made. The ideas and information in Chapters 5 and 6 are critical to any understanding of the debates involved in the study of crime and deviance. Attempts to answer examination essay questions that do not show evidence of knowledge and evaluations of the sociological debates will be dismissed as being mere common sense.

Group Work

1   This can also be done as an individual exercise, or you may need to tailor the amount of research depending on the number of people in your class. Each group should take on one sociological perspective. Each member of the group should then try and find the names of three or four researchers and writers within their chosen tradition.

Use a number of your textbooks including this one. Write down the following summary information about your chosen studies and theories:

* author
* date
* perspective
* twenty words or so summarising the main conclusion offered.

Pool your results within the group and then within the whole class. Use the information to create a time line for the studies and perspectives you have chosen. Try and identify themes and areas of concern noting how they change in the study of criminology over the decades.

This should give each of you a simple overview of the movement of the debate within the subject and will provide you all with an essay list of studies to cite in support of your arguments under examination conditions.

As a simple tip, this is work that is made very much easier with the use of computers. If you print your information in a table format, it can be sorted by date of publication by using the 'sort' option under the 'table' format heading.

2   Organise a discussion exercise around the idea that 'Criminology without theory has no point or value'. Make notes both for and against the motion.

Coursework

Chapters 5 and 6 are highly theoretical. If you are attempting coursework on a theme related to the study of crime and deviance, then the contents of these chapters should inform all of your work. This discussion is particularly relevant to your context section. To produce a piece of coursework that is particularly designed to show understanding and evaluation of the theory that you have covered in the previous two chapters can be a complex task. You are strongly advised not to attempt work that is too ambitious for you to manage successfully in the time available. Take the advice of your teacher.

There is one methodological approach that can lend itself to highly analytical styles of working and which can be undertaken in a relatively short piece of writing. This is the case study. There are two possible ways to attempt a case study when looking at crime and social reactions to it.

1 *'A case study of decision-making in a Crown Court'*
   Go to a Crown Court and observe a case. This is easily arranged though for courtesy you should write to the clerk of the court for permission and to explain your activity. Check how long the trial will last because some trials can last for several days. Make detailed notes of the evidence and the court practice.

   You are not concerned with the guilt or motivations of the defendant but with the processes that you see about how courts operate, the assumptions made by lawyers and the defences that are offered in mitigation. Discuss the observations that you have made about the case with specific and continual reference to social theory. Look for issues of class, ethnicity, gender, disability, morality, social values and the nature of the criminal act.

2 *'Media reporting of criminal cases'*
   Collect as much data as possible about a particular court case that is well covered by both tabloid and broadsheet newspapers. This could be historical but then you will need the cooperation of a good public librarian as well as plenty of photocopying money and access to CD-Rom newspapers. Do not be distracted by the details of the events of the case itself or you may simply produce a gruesome and unpleasant scrapbook. Again, you must avoid making judgements as to the possible guilt or motivation of the defendant or you will not be analysing your material sociologically.

   Look for issues of class, ethnicity, gender, disability, morality, social values and the nature of the criminal act in the reporting. What kind of language is used to discuss the witnesses and the defendant? What important moral issues do the newspapers raise? What assumptions about the nature of the crime and the criminal are made? Talk to the people around you and ask them for their views. What social attitudes and beliefs about the general nature of crime and criminality are revealed in their responses?

You have already been advised to reread this and Chapter 5 continuously. There are other simple tips for you to ensure that you fully understand the debates. The examining boards expect that you should be able to apply your understanding of sociology to the social world around you. There are different ways of doing this:

1 Train yourself to think sociologically and begin to question events that are going on around you. Ask yourself about why people make the assumptions that they do about crime. Relate the ideas that people have to the theoretical understandings that you have gained from your study.

2 Watch documentary programmes about crime on television. Think about what you see in a sociological manner and apply theory. What assumptions about the culture and social activities of criminals are held in common by the programme makers? What is revealed about the nature of our culture and the assumptions that are made about crime and criminal behaviour?

3 Analyse fictional programmes about crime. What motives do the criminals have for their actions? How do the programme makers present criminals? What stereotypes and social constructions can you observe in the programmes?

4 Develop your synoptic understanding by revising all that you can about the perspectives as they are applied in other areas of study from your syllabus. How do these other topics relate to the study of crime and criminality?

5 Ensure that you are up-to-date with public debate about crime, criminal law and social order by looking at broadsheet newspapers and listening to current affairs programmes on Radio 4. The Today Programme in the morning is particularly good. Do not expect to follow what is happening immediately; it takes time to develop an understanding and awareness of current events, so the sooner you start the better.

1 *Assess the importance of feminism in understanding crime in our society.*
This is another 'catch-all' type of question because you can substitute any type of theory or any writer for the word 'feminism'. You are advised therefore to prepare yourself for this type of question by making sure that you have notes that satisfactorily answer the question of how useful any perspective is. It is these processes of analysis and evaluation which make up the most significant assessment targets in the examination. List the advantages and disadvantages of each perspective and make a note of the criticisms and evaluations that are offered to you in this text.

You would be ill-advised to reject feminism totally for this essay because it offers a whole new set of insights into criminology. This leaves you with two possible options for answering the question:

- Point out the shortcomings of previous theorising and then praise the feminism for its critical approach to malestream knowledge. This is the safer option for a candidate who feels insecure in the knowledge base, as a short overview of the whole debate is all that is necessary. The main danger is that the candidate will become descriptive and will not actually consider feminism itself in enough detail to satisfy an examiner.

- Develop a balanced argument which is entirely based on an understanding of feminism and which offers an understanding of its strengths and shortcomings as a perspective. This demands a good understanding of what it is that feminist writers are trying to achieve in their work. The candidate will have to consider the obvious strengths of feminism and refer to feminist theory and debate within the perspective itself. A critical approach is necessary towards any question based on essay writing and some of the shortcomings of feminism will need to be considered. These will probably focus on empirical questions of the value-laden nature of feminism. Feminism does not attempt to be objective or scientific, concerned as it is with meaning and understanding. However, for those who consider sociology to be a science-based subject, this approach is also its weakness.

2 Substitute Marxism for *feminism* in question 1 and use the advice given to construct your answer.

7

SUICIDE: THE ULTIMATE DEVIANCE

Introduction

PREVIOUS CHAPTERS IN this books have focused predominantly on crime as an example of deviant behaviour. In this chapter, we focus on suicide as an act of deviance that is so extreme that there can be no after word, retribution or apology if it is successful.

Whilst suicide is no longer a criminal act in Britain, it can be considered deviant behaviour in the sense that it goes against both the moral and ethical teachings of religion and culture. It can also be argued that it goes against the natural instincts of most people who will struggle to survive, and thus it breaks all cultural norms and values. In this chapter, we will consider definitions of suicide, the inadequacy of official suicide statistics and evaluate functionalist and interpretivist perspectives which attempt to explain suicide. Whilst new material is introduced in this chapter, the study of suicide can be considered a case study to revise earlier themes and consolidate your understanding of key issues relevant to the sociology of crime and deviance.

DEFINING SUICIDE

What is suicide? In Britain, suicide and attempted suicide were criminal offences until 1961. Now the act is no longer defined as a violation of the criminal law, but it is often viewed as deviant, and accorded shame. Look at the following definition, which the *Oxford English Reference Dictionary* (1986) offers:

1 the intentional killing of oneself; an instance of this; a person who does
2 an action destructive to one's own interests or reputation.

Table 11: *Theorists, concepts and issues in this chapter*		
KEY THEORISTS	KEY CONCEPTS	KEY ISSUES
Durkheim	Egoism Anomie Altruism Fatalism Moral regulation Social integration	Suicide is a social action based on the degree of integration and regulation between individuals and society.
Douglas Atkinson	Meanings Social construction	Statistics merely reflect common assumptions about an act and offer little insight about personal meanings. Suicide is a social construct with coroners as key players in the definition of an act as suicide.
Taylor Giddens	Realism (Taylor) Structuration (Giddens)	Studies of suicide need to take into account a sense of meaning the act has for the individual but also consider structural factors.

This dictionary definition raises more questions than it answers:

- How do we know whether an individual intended to kill him or herself?
- Is the act of suicide always regarded as destructive?

We will consider these questions in turn. Later in this chapter we will explore the work of interpretivists who argue that the concept of suicide is socially constructed. They point out that not only does the meaning of suicide vary between different cultures and different historical periods, but what becomes defined as suicide depends on the meanings social actors attach to a particular act. It is not always clear that the individual intended to kill him or herself and thus people must interpret the events based on the evidence available to them. The actor is dead and cannot be quizzed as to the nature of his or her intentions.

OFFICIAL SUICIDE VERDICTS

Jones (1998) gives two examples of acts that were officially defined as suicide:

1 The death of 39 members of the Californian religious cult, Heaven's Gate, who apparently willingly took their own lives by taking a toxic cocktail of barbiturates, alcohol and a sweet sauce in 1997. They participated in this mass

suicide because they believed they would attain a new life on another planet. The coroner's report showed evidence that some of the deaths were a result of suffocation and thus were assisted suicides.

2   The death of Michael Hutchence, the lead singer of INXS, who was found in his Australian hotel bedroom hanging by a belt in 1998. Although it appears a classic scenario of suicide, the verdict was challenged because he was seen in the company of some young actresses shortly before his death and so a possible accidental death from some group-sex act was inferred. This challenge was overridden once evidence of depression and anxiety were presented.

In these two instances, the evidence is far from clear-cut and alternative verdicts were possible such as unlawful killing (case 1) or accidental death (case 2).

Activity

There have been a number of notable deaths or suicides of famous celebrities such as Marilyn Monroe and Kurt Cobain. Talk to people you know about these celebrities and consult biographies on them. What stories have grown up around the deaths of some of these people? Are there any cases where the cause of death remains a matter of controversy?

SUICIDE IN DIFFERENT CULTURES

Viewing suicide as a destructive act is not universal. The act of taking one's own life has different meanings for members of different societies. For example, among Trobriand Islanders, attempted suicide is used as an acceptable sanction in matrimonial disputes and is regarded as an indictment of an offending spouse. In Japan, suicide is often regarded as an honourable death and may become a complex ceremony for the victim. During the Second World War, many Japanese pilots were desperate for the privilege of piloting suicide planes against US warships. This self-sacrifice was known as kamikaze. One pilot was rejected for the training because he was a husband and father. His wife then drowned herself and their children in order to allow her husband the great honour of becoming the last suicide pilot to die in the war.

Activity

Use CD-Rom, history and anthropology texts or encyclopaedias to investigate suicide customs and death rituals in other cultures. You are advised to look up under suttee, hari-kiri and kamikaze.

DURKHEIM'S DEFINITION OF SUICIDE

The classic study is *Suicide* and it was first published in 1897. It was written by Emile Durkheim, working within the functionalist tradition, and it is important because it helped to establish the use of official statistics by sociologists to empirically test theories. We discuss this work in detail later in the chapter but at this stage it is helpful to consider Durkheim's definition of suicide because it illustrates the different types of behaviours which can be labelled suicide and how suicide is not always seen as a shameful act.

... every case of death resulting directly or indirectly from a positive or negative act performed by the victim which he knows will produce this result

Durkheim 1897

A positive act might be regarded as hanging oneself. A negative act might be the captain who goes down with the ship (Bilton et al 1987). In Britain and many other countries, it is expected that senior officers should not leave a ship until everyone has left. This may be seen as a heroic act to save the lives of others.

Study point
Can you think of a number of social situations in which people are expected to put their own lives at risk or to avoid protecting themselves for the sake of other people?

Studying suicide therefore illustrates how the categories of crime and deviance are socially constructed and thus culturally and historically relative. The question of how suicide may be defined is one of the key sociological debates, dividing functionalists and interpretivists. Marxism and other sociological perspectives seem to have less to say on the topic. The next area of debate to consider is the usefulness of official suicide statistics.

MEASURING SUICIDE

Only a small minority of people deliberately end their own lives. We are not certain how many take the attempt. About 1 per cent of all deaths in Britain are officially classified as suicides (Bilton et al 1987). This figure is open to debate, however, as the following discussions will show.

Official statistics suggest that particular groups are more at risk of committing suicide than others. Young men are most at risk. For those aged 15–24, after road accidents, suicide is the next most common cause of death and accounts for the

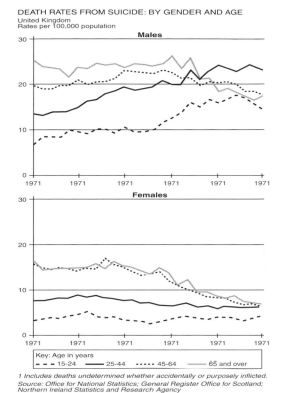

DEATH RATES FROM SUICIDE: BY GENDER AND AGE
United Kingdom
Rates per 100,000 population

Males

Females

Key: Age in years
- - - 15-24   —— 25-44   ····· 45-64   —— 65 and over

1 Includes deaths undetermined whether accidentally or purposely inflicted.
Source: Office for National Statistics; General Register Office for Scotland;
Northern Ireland Statistics and Research Agency

DEATH RATES FROM SUICIDE: BY GENDER AND AGE

fifth of all deaths (Jones 1998). This pattern seems similar across Europe. Suicide rates among men are higher than for women in all age groups. Among those aged 25–44, men were almost four times more likely than women to commit suicide in 1996 while among those aged 45 and over, men were more than twice as likely as women to do so (*Social Trends* 1997).

There are a number of risk factors thought to influence the likelihood of a person committing suicide (*Social Trends* 1997). These include:

- marital status (those who are single or divorced are more likely to commit suicide)
- alcohol and drug misuse (the risk is particularly increased for men aged 15–24)
- occupational status (between 1979 and 1990 men who worked as pharmacists, dentists, farmers, doctors or vets were most at risk).

Precisely because of the apparent 'fact' that suicide can be linked to social factors, Durkheim argues that we cannot understand why suicide is a feature of modern life by means of a study of individual cases.

EXPLAINING SUICIDE

FUNCTIONALIST APPROACHES

Durkheim is one of the founding fathers of the functionalist tradition. He argues that sociology was the study of society and not of individuals. Thus whilst society is made up of individuals, society is something more than the mere sum of those individuals. People are born into societies which are already organised with rules, values and norms which shape and influence people's behaviour in ways that they may not always realise. Thus the task Durkheim set himself in *Suicide* was to demonstrate that even the supremely and seemingly individual act of suicide was influenced by society.

In *Rules of Sociological Method* (1895), Durkheim set out some methodological prescriptions. The best-known of his rules is that sociologists should treat social facts as if they were *things*. Social facts, he argues, have two properties:

1 They are external to individuals and they exercise constraint over the individual.
2 Social facts are observable and capable of scientific measurement.

Applied to suicide, Durkheim argued that the suicide rate was a social fact and in common with other social facts could be observed and measured. In order to do this, he used officially produced suicide statistics as his basis of analysis. From his statistical analysis, Durkheim drew three conclusions:

1 Within single societies the incidence or rate of suicide remains remarkably constant over time.
2 The suicide rate varies between countries.
3 The suicide rate varies between different groups in the same society.

Based on these conclusions, Durkheim developed his sociological explanation of suicide. It is based on two key concepts: **social integration** and **moral regulation**. According to Durkheim, society constrains individuals in two ways:

1 It integrates them by binding them to the values and norms of social groups.
2 It regulates their potentially limitless desires and aspirations by defining specific goals and means of attaining them.

Without integration and regulation, human life would be chaotic and society would experience social disorder. Deviant or pathological trends such as suicide, he believed, could be explained in terms of the lack of integration or regulation of the individual in society.

For Durkheim, suicide varies with the degree of integration and regulation of the social group of which the individual forms a part. Based on this proposition, he classified suicide into four types:

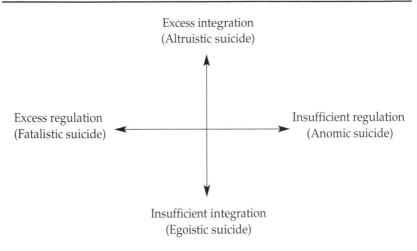

Excess integration
(Altruistic suicide)

Excess regulation
(Fatalistic suicide)

Insufficient regulation
(Anomic suicide)

Insufficient integration
(Egoistic suicide)

SUICIDE TYPES AND THE BALANCE OF SOCIETY (LEE AND NEWBY 1983)

TYPES OF SUICIDE

Egoistic suicide

This form of suicide is the product of insufficient integration and is a feature of modern societies. Durkheim offered the following evidence to support his view. Suicide rates vary according to religious affiliation, marital status and political events:

- The suicide rate is higher among Protestants than Catholics because Protestantism tolerates individualism and free enquiry into the basis of religious belief. In contrast to Catholics, Protestants are less likely to be closely integrated into a religious group.
- Rates of suicide are higher among those not integrated into a family, eg bachelors and the widowed.
- Suicide rates are lower during wartime and political unrest because the situation brings people together.

Greater integration can be viewed as a strategy to prevent suicide but Durkheim warned of the dangers of excessive integration.

Altruistic suicide

Altruism is the act of putting others before oneself. Altruistic suicide is found mainly in traditional or primitive societies. Durkheim suggested that if there is too much integration, individuals may feel a sense of overwhelming moral obligation to kill themselves in response to particular events and to uphold the values of their culture. An example of this might include societies where the bereaved wife is expected to kill herself following her husband's death.

Anomic suicide

This is by far the most interesting discussion because it illustrates many of the ideas that underlie Durkheim's thinking. Anomic suicide is related to the lack of regulation in modern societies. He suggested that when society becomes unpredictable, people lose their sense of social belonging and understanding. They become distressed. To illustrate his argument, Durkheim refers to his findings that individuals are more likely to kill themselves in times of economic recession. The concept of anomie is crucial to Durkheim's work. He refers to anomie in two different ways in his writings (Lee and Newby 1983):

1 The absence of regulation or rules so that the parts of the social order are insufficiently coordinated, for instance, during periods of economic depression. In this sense, he views anomie as a property of society.
2 The consequence of anomie in society for individuals is to create a sense of isolation and meaninglessness of life and work. Individuals are thus more likely to commit suicide but their psychological state reflects the condition of society as a whole.

He also refers to anomie in domestic contexts and refers to the higher suicide rate amongst the divorced and separated compared to the married.

Study point

What are the similarities and the differences between the Durkheimian concept of anomie and the Marxist concept of alienation?

Fatalistic suicide

Durkheim only mentions this type of suicide in a brief footnote and no examples are provided. Fatalistic suicide is the product of excessive regulation and is the counterpart of altruistic suicide. It might be the act of one who no longer cares or feels that she or he cannot do anything to affect events.

Activity

How useful is Durkheim's analysis of suicide when applied to the passage below?

For example, at Pine Ridge, a 5,000 square mile reservation in south-western South Dakota on which 18,000 (American) Indians live, more than eight out of ten adults are unemployed, and many are alcoholics. As a result of these conditions, the suicide rate on the reservation is up to four times the national average.

Tischler, 1996

DURKHEIM'S INFLUENCE ON SOCIOLOGY

A number of characteristics of Durkheim's work have influenced sociologists (Abercrombie et al 1994). These include:

- A belief that suicide rates can be related to social contexts, in particular, levels of social integration.
- A concern with aggregate suicide rates, rather than individual acts and motives.
- A positivistic approach that relates suicide rates to 'objective' external variables.
- The use of government statistics as a data source.

Durkheim's work has been favourably received. For example, Merton (1957) describes *Suicide* as perhaps the greatest piece of sociological research ever done. However, it has also been criticised on a number of grounds, both methodological and theoretical. **Bilton** et al (1987) suggest that Durkheim's work has been subjected to both internal critiques from those working in the functionalist tradition, which we discuss now, and external critiques by interpretivists. As a word of warning, despite the criticisms that are offered below of Durkheim's work, you would be unwise to dismiss it entirely since much of what was said remains relevant today.

Points of evaluation

1 **Halbwachs** (1930) was a student of Durkheim. He suggested that in order to explain suicide rates we should not try to isolate single social factors such as religious beliefs or marital status, but focus on how social factors combine in conditions of modern life to make some social groups more vulnerable to suicide than others. In sum, he argued for a more complex explanation of suicide which avoids simplistic causal statements.
2 **Gibbs** and **Martin** (1964) argue that Durkheim's work can be criticised because he failed to define adequately one of his key concepts – social integration.
3 **Pope** (1976) suggested that Durkheim ignored data which did not fit his hypothesis.

It is these criticisms which have provided the basis for interpretivist analyses. The interpretivist critique focuses on how we define the term suicide and the usefulness of using suicide rates as a basis for a sociological explanation of the phenomenon.

INTERPRETATIVE APPROACHES

Interpretivists question some of the basic assumptions that underlie Durkheim's work. They argue that the source of individual behaviour cannot be seen as external to individual actors. This is because social reality is actively created by individuals who mean to do things and attribute meaning to the behaviour of others. These meanings are not necessarily shared in the unproblematic way functionalists assume.

Applying this theoretical framework to suicide, we can challenge the Durkheimian position that suicide is an easily recognised form of behaviour that can be studied using official suicide statistics. A more critical position is to suggest that suicide rates are socially constructed: definitions and collection procedures of officials will vary and suicide rates can be considered biased because they only represent a sample of suicidal actions. The task for sociologists should be to explain how deaths become defined as 'suicides' or to explain suicide by using alternative data sources. The focus of interpretivists has been on the former task. We now examine the key works of **Douglas** (1967) and **Atkinson** (1978).

The Social Meaning of Suicide (Douglas 1967)

Douglas suggests that Durkheim's work is fundamentally flawed because he relies on official suicide rates. Douglas suggests these rates are systematically biased. For example, the more socially integrated a community, the more likely they are to conceal suicides for a number of reasons:

1 Relatives and friends will make a greater attempt to hide evidence of suicide.
2 Officials may be less likely to recognise and record the death as suicide if an individual died in a way that is open to interpretation and where the evidence remains doubtful.

Discovering Suicide (Atkinson 1978)

Atkinson's work looks at coroners' reports and explores the ways in which they decide whether deaths are suicides. He argues that there are certain pieces of evidence that are taken by coroners as indicators of suicidal intent. These include primary suicidal cues from the scene of the death and secondary suicidal cues from the life history of the deceased.

Primary Cues

* manner of death
* suicide note.

Secondary Cues

* state of mind and behaviour prior to death
* suicidal motive.

Many cases will not be clear-cut and there may be conflicting evidence 'for' and 'against' suicidal intent. The coroner has to make a verdict consistent with general cultural assumptions about suicide.

What these two pieces of work have in common is a belief that suicide rates cannot be taken at face value and used as a basis of a sociological explanation.

Activity
Suggest reasons why courts may be unwilling to classify a death, especially of a young person, as a suicide.

COMBINING FUNCTIONALIST AND INTERPRETATIVE APPROACHES

The study of suicide, like the study of crime, illustrates the problem of 'structure' and 'action' in sociological analyses. It would be foolish to deny the influence of the social environment upon individuals but at the same time human beings are not simply robots, passively responding to structural forces: they make meaningful choices. Consequently, some theorists have tried to combine different theoretical approaches.

Taylor (1988) suggests that Durkheim was aware of the social construction of suicide statistics but felt they were important in the search for broad patterns. In this sense, he can be described as a realist. Taylor has developed Durkheim's typology of suicide in an attempt to inject a concern with meaning into Durkheimian perspective.

Similarly, **Giddens** argues that sociologists need to explore the relationship between social forces and individual motives in order to adequately explain the phenomenon of suicide or, indeed, any social phenomenon. In later works, Giddens (1984) describes this as **structuration theory**, a framework which can be applied to any social phenomenon.

SUMMARY

Studying suicide highlights many of the sociological debates we have discussed in earlier chapters. As sociologists we need to be aware that suicide is a social construct and that official data on suicide is the product of social interaction. Sociologists disagree about the causes of suicide. Those adopting a structural approach, such as Durkheim, focus on the influence of the social environment upon individuals. In contrast, interpretivists, including Douglas and Atkinson, argue that it is wrong to view humans as passively responding to social forces and suggest the need to recognise individual motives for suicidal behaviour. Others have adopted a midway position (Giddens 1977, Taylor 1988) and attempt to synthesise functionalism and interpretivism.

Key Concept Activity

Look at the following terms and be sure that you understand their meaning. Use them in your examination work:

- functionalism
- social facts
- interpretivism
- anomie
- egoistic suicide
- altruistic suicide.

Group Work

1 Look up the following Web site for more detailed statistical information to supplement the information in this chapter: http://www.samaritans.org.uk In addition to sensible advice on how to deal with someone you think may be suicidal, there is a wealth of statistical data on suicide rates and patterns presented in a user-friendly and easy to access format.
2 If you do not have access to Web sites, write to the local branch of The Samaritans and ask for any information they have on suicide rates and patterns.

Coursework

If you were contemplating a study of suicide or of suicide attempts as part of your A Level coursework, the simplest advice is, 'Don't'. This topic is totally unsuited to any but the most skilled of researchers:

- Suicide is, arguably, one of the most terrible forms of death for close family members in our society to have to come to terms with and they will not welcome your probing. You may do untold damage to people even if they profess willingness to help.
- If you have an interest in suicide because you have some personal experience of this form of death, then you may be tempted to use your coursework as a form of self-therapy. This is entirely inappropriate for the purposes of the examination.
- Relying on official statistics for analysis is unreliable for all of the reasons outlined in the chapter.
- Adopting a qualitative approach is also problematic.

Revision Hints

Suicide is an important topic area and you should be aware of the underlying significance of the debate. However, you are advised that it rarely crops up in examination papers two years in a row. This is where a study of the pattern of questions from your examination board over a period of years will be particularly useful. If a question has not appeared for a couple of years, be certain that you know the suicide discussions well. Otherwise, be aware of the topic, but concentrate on more regular question areas such as the official statistics debate and you can then refer to the issues surrounding the collection of data regarding suicide for your evidence.

Very many poor answers will be submitted to examiners on this topic despite the fact that many of the candidates will know the subject well. This is because many people will write descriptive essays based on knowledge and they will simply regurgitate their lesson notes and reading without thought. Organise your revision in this topic area around the debates so that you can analyse the contributions of the various studies to the development of sociology and criminology as a whole:

- Why is suicide deviant?
- Why did Durkheim study suicide?
- What insight does this study offer to later researchers?
- How did Durkheim study suicide?
- What strengths and criticisms can you note about Durkheim's methodology?
- What does Douglas add to the debate?
- What did Atkinson add to the debate?
- What did Steve Taylor do to reconcile functionalism and interpretivism?
- What personal perspective can you bring to the debate?

Exam Hints

Evaluate the suggestion that Durkheim has little to tell us about the causes of suicide in contemporary society.

Despite the many critical analyses of Durkheim's work, and recent rejections of functionalism as a perspective, it still remains today an enormously useful starting point for discussion. Do not be distracted under examination conditions into personal accounts or viewpoints on the causes of suicide. In sociology, the debate is about the social origin of the act and not the personal impact. You may find yourself diverted into a psychological analysis unless you are very selective in your commentary. The arguments you should use must focus on the debate between meaning (interpretivism) and statistical analysis (functionalism) and from these perspectives, Marxists generally have little to add to the discussion.

8

CONTROLLING CRIME

Introduction

IN CHAPTERS 5 and 6 we explored a wide range of theoretical perspectives each of which attempted to explain criminal behaviour. These perspectives offer different views on how offenders should be dealt with, and the ways in which crime can be prevented. This may be a good point at which to revisit your study notes and to consider how the different perspectives suggest society should deal with the problem of crime. The relationship between sociological perspectives and social policy making is a significant element of the A Level syllabus.

In this chapter we focus our attention on strategies of crime control and its links with social control. We do not consider in detail the working of criminal justice agencies although suitable texts are recommended at the end of the book, where you will also find a diagram of the criminal justice system in England and Wales. Rather, the aim is to explore the historical development of criminal justice and consider contemporary responses to crime, particularly in the late twentieth century.

CRIME CONTROL AND SOCIAL CONTROL

In this chapter, we consider both crime control and social control. **Crime control** refers to organised and official responses to crime which generally focus on identifying and dealing with offenders (those officially labelled criminal). This form of control is exercised by the State through criminal justice agencies such as the police, the courts, the prison service and the probation service. You should note that only a minority of those who offend are subject to criminal sanctions, or punishment.

Table 12: *Theorists, concepts and issues in this chapter*		
KEY THEORISTS	KEY CONCEPTS	KEY ISSUES
Whig historians	Justice Social change as progressive	The history of the criminal justice system is one of increasing fairness and equality.
Revisionist historians	State Power relations Economic interests	Reform of the criminal justice system has extended State power and control.
Gelsthorpe	What is justice?	Justice is a contested concept.
Foucault Cohen Shearing and Stenning	Social control Netwidening Surveillance	Social control now expands into all areas of life.
Left realism	Relative deprivation Political marginalisation Social crime prevention Multi-agency work Community safety	Crime is a social problem with far-reaching effects. Society needs to support victims and encourage collaboration between the criminal justice system and welfare agencies to deal with crime.
Right realism	Individual processes Rational choice Deterrence Situational crime prevention	To deal with the problem of crime, we need to deter offenders through harsh sentences and crime prevention strategies.

Home Office statisticians (Barclay 1995) estimate that an offender is convicted by the criminal courts or receives a police caution for only 3 in 100 offences committed.

Agencies of socialisation, such as the family and education systems, have an important role to play in the prevention of particular crimes, usually the most visible crimes, and in this way affect the lives of everyone. Consequently, the study of crime control cannot be separated from the study of social control.

Social control is to do with the overall means by which social conformity and regulation are secured. Its affects all members of society, not just those officially labelled criminals. Sociologists often make a distinction between formal and informal social control:

- **Formal social control** involves control being exercised by State agencies over the lives of individuals.

- **Informal social control** is exercised by a wide range of institutions including the family, religion, the peer group and education. These institutions are agencies of social control and have powerful effects on the behaviour of individuals.

Agencies such as the family can prevent individuals committing crime. Feminists have noted that the greater social control women experience in the home is one explanation for low levels of offending by women (see Chapter 6). Conversely, some agencies of socialisation can also encourage individuals to commit criminal acts. For instance, sub-cultural theorists (see Chapter 5) have noted the importance of the peer group in determining criminal behaviour and extensive research has explored the relationship between family background and crime (see Farrington 1997).

Activity
Imagine you were guilty of causing death through drunken driving. What would be the possible social effects on you of such a conviction? Think of both legal and social effects. Make a 'brainstorm' diagram. Whose reaction to such a conviction would you fear most; the legal sanctions from the law or the social sanctions from your family and friends? Compare your responses with friends of the opposite gender. Do different patterns emerge within the group for males and females?

SOCIAL CONTROL AS A CONTEST CONCEPT

The different sociological perspectives you have been introduced to in this text have different views of the nature of social control in society because they have different views on how society is organised:

- Functionalists define it as a process by which deviant behaviour is counteracted and social stability maintained through the imposition of sanctions.
- Interactionists refer to social control as the process by which stability of social groups, community relations and shared values are sustained, usually without recourse to coercive and authoritarian discipline. They also highlight how coercive social control tends to amplify deviance rather than diminish it (see Chapter 6).
- Marxists argue that social control can be defined in terms of coercion of the proletariat by the bourgeoisie.
- Feminists emphasise the gendered nature of social control and note how ideologies of conformity and structures of control successfully regulate and discipline women. For examples, ideologies which surround sexual behaviour permit, and perhaps even admire, sexual permissiveness in men but label

women who engage in the same behaviours as 'sluts' or 'slags' (Lees 1986, 1993). Structures of control include the family and peer pressure.

Whilst sociologists have different definitions of social control, the majority believe it can be achieved through a combination of compliance, coercion and commitment to social values (Abercrombie et al 1994).

Study point

Consider the different theoretical perspectives and their (a) definitions of social control and (b) their views on how society is organised. Which do you agree with? Which one do you think most politicians would agree with?

In the next section, we explore the historical development of the criminal justice system and note the changing nature of crime control.

THE HISTORICAL DEVELOPMENT OF THE CRIMINAL JUSTICE SYSTEM

In this section, we explore briefly the historical development of the criminal justice system, focusing predominantly on England and Wales. You should be aware that criminal processes, and much of the criminal law, are different in Scotland (Young and Young 1994) and Northern Ireland (Dickson 1989). This is largely for historical reasons.

METHODOLOGICAL ISSUES

Sharpe (1996) offers two main reasons for studying the history of the criminal justice system:

1 Current debates about crime and crime control all too easily slide into contrasting our present situation with some earlier 'golden age' in which the problem of crime was less serious and under control. Historical study allows informed comment on these debates.
2 Historical study allows us to contrast our own ways of thinking about and dealing with the problem of crime with past responses based on different assumptions.

You should be aware that there are different perspectives that characterise the academic discipline of history. Historians, like sociologists, disagree about how best to gather, conceptualise and analyse their data. This is illustrated in later discussion of the emergence of the prison system.

THE PROFESSIONALISATION OF THE CRIMINAL JUSTICE SYSTEM

As **Emsley** (1997) notes, the system of prosecution and activity within the courtroom increasingly became the preserve of experts and professionals from the mid-eighteenth century. Throughout the eighteenth century, the decision to prosecute an offender in England and Wales was generally taken by the victim or by the victim's relations or friends. Whilst in Scotland the State became involved in the prosecution of serious crime, government officials in England and Wales rarely intervened. However, as the nineteenth century wore on, the police in England and Wales increasingly took on the role of prosecutor. The police force was emerging at this time as a professional and centralised body (Emsley 1996). Decisions to prosecute are no longer made by the Police, but by the Crown Prosecution Service which was created in 1985.

Activity
The Crown Prosecution Service is able to send out useful information packs to interested individuals. The current address of the CPS is 50 Ludgate Hill, London EC4M 7EX (0171 334 8505). The Web site offers both English and Welsh language versions at http://www.cps.gov.uk.

The existence of the criminal courts has a long history. Currently, there are three main types of criminal courts, although there are others such as the Court of Appeal:

1 **Magistrates' Courts:** dating back to the eighteenth century, these are courts which deal with the less serious offences, approximately 98 per cent of cases.
2 **Crown Courts**: created by the 1971 Courts Act, these deal with the most serious offences.
3 **Youth Courts**: these were created by the 1991 Criminal Justice Act, although juvenile courts have existed since 1908. They hear cases where the defendants are aged between 10 and 17.

WHAT IS CRIMINAL JUSTICE?

The aim of the courts is to deliver criminal justice but there are different views about what criminal justice actually is. Gelsthorpe (1996) discusses five perspectives on criminal justice. Criminal justice systems are likely to combine elements of these different perspectives.

Table 13: *Five perspectives on criminal justice*	
PERSPECTIVE ON JUSTICE	KEY IDEAS
1 Due Process	Justice needs to be administered according to legal rules and procedures that are publicly known, fair and seen to be just.
2 Crime Control	The primary function of the criminal courts is to punish offenders and, by so doing, to control crime.
3 Welfare and Rehabilitative	The aim of criminal justice is to diagnose, treat and cure offenders.
4 Power and Domination	Criminal justice is a means of legitimating and maintaining class and other forms of domination.
5 Managerial and Bureaucratic	The criminal justice system is a set of bureaucracies governed by rules and routines whose role is to manage the problem of crime.

DELIVERING JUSTICE

Increasingly, the ability of the courts to deliver justice (however it is defined) is being questioned. In the late 1980s, there was an unusual level of anxiety provoked by extreme miscarriages of justice. This was marked by a number of television programmes and dramatised films which documented such cases and the impact that they had on the victims. Many of the cases that provoked the most serious public concern had a political element in that they were linked to the treatment of suspects in terrorist offences by the IRA. Other cases, however, seemed to point to police misconduct and incompetence or to gross inequities, political and social bias in the law itself.

Activity

Consider a case of miscarriage of justice. Past examples include the Guildford Four, the Birmingham Six and Derek Bentley (see Rozenberg 1992).

What issues does the particular case you have chosen raise about the operation of criminal justice generally?

Gelsthorpe (1996) suggests that there are a number of controversies that surround critical decision and processes in the courts. The questions she poses are discussed below:

Is there disparity in sentencing?

Magistrates and judges have considerable discretion in sentencing, although there are guidelines which have to be followed. Decisions are based not only on the seriousness of the offence but on the individual circumstance of the offender. Whilst this aspect has been celebrated by criminal justice professionals, critics have noted regional variations (Liberty 1992). It also introduces potential for differential treatment of different social groups (see Chapter 4).

Are judges and magistrates impartial?

Critics have questioned the impartiality of the judges and magistrates because they only represent a particular section of society and are often seen as 'out of touch'. Magistrates are usually white, middle-aged and middle-class. It is no longer fair to say that they are predominantly male. However, most judges are male and the typical judge is middle-aged or older, white and with a public school and/or 'Oxbridge' background.

Is trial by jury fair?

Trial by jury is one of the oldest aspects of the legal process. A jury consists of 12 members of the public who are over 18. They witness the trial and then are allowed time to discuss the case and to decide whether the defendant is guilty or innocent. Juries are only involved in Crown Court cases and they have no role in sentencing decisions. Opinion on their value is divided. Whilst some see the importance of public input as crucial, others see them as out of place and question the ability of juries to deal with complex cases.

Activity
Organise a debate around one of the three questions raised by Gelsthorpe.

These questions relate to a central question: is the criminal justice system imbued with discriminatory attitudes and practices? As we discussed in Chapter 4, there is substantial evidence to suggest that particular groups do receive different treatment at the hands of criminal justice agencies. Certainly, the criminal justice system is not representative of the social make-up of society in terms of class, gender, ethnicity and other divisions. Moreover, criminal justice does not operate in a vacuum and therefore is likely to represent discriminatory attitudes and practices in wider society.

Activity

Most trials are completely open to the public and you are advised to spend a day
witnessing a Magistrates Court in session and a day viewing a Crown Court trial.
Controversial trials may have limited seating available, but usually members of the
public are entitled to walk in and out of court as they please. For courtesy, write to the
Clerk of the Court if you wish to go with a group of people. They may be able to
organise guided visits.

THE CHANGING NATURE OF SOCIAL CONTROL

PRISONS

The history of prisons is marked by competing versions of events. 'Whig'
histories, based on the accounts of reformers rather than prisoners, have tended
to celebrate reform as improvement. Whig history refers to a view of history that
is similar to modernism in sociology (see Chapter 9). It implies a continual
progression and improvement in society as a result of parliamentary democracy
and should not be confused with the historical political party of the same name.
Whig historians saw the use of imprisonment as progressive, when compared to
capital punishment, for example. This historical perspective is no longer the
standard position. In contrast, revisionist historians have retold the story in the
context of economic interest, power relations and the role of the State. Reform
was seen as an extension of structures of centralised power and control.

Marxists such as **Ignatieff** (1978) have highlighted how the development of the
prison coincided with the development of industrial capitalism and was linked to
the need to maintain social order. Perhaps the most influential has been the work
of **Foucault** (1977). Key points of his argument include:

1 Since the 'birth' of the prison around the turn of the nineteenth century,
   punishment is no longer aimed at the body (compared with capital
   punishment) but aimed towards training the human soul. He describes this as
   the 'great transformation'.
2 Within the prison, ideas and knowledge (eg the disciplines of psychology and
   psychiatry) act as a form of disciplinary power and as a form of social control
   over individuals.
3 Techniques of supervision and surveillance first formulated in the prison have
   penetrated the whole of society such that we are all subject to social control,
   although we may not realise it.

Foucault's work is directed at developments of penal practice in the nineteenth century but many criminologists have applied his theoretical framework to social control in the late twentieth century.

Cohen's (1985) influential text entitled *Visions of Social Control* draws on many of Foucault's ideas. He suggests that there has been a proliferation and elaboration of other forms of social control, which coexist alongside the prison. Using a series of metaphors, he analyses the changes that he claims account to a reversal of the great transformation:

- **Widening the net**: new strategies to deal with crime often increase the number of people subject to formal social control. For example, the introduction of new community penalties such as electronic monitoring ('tagging') may be used for people who would previously have received a fine. Additionally, programmes may target those at risk of offending rather than those who offend. For instance, the Crime and Disorder Act (1998) has powers to subject children at risk of offending to curfew orders.
- **Thinning the mesh**: offenders are subject to increasing intervention. For example, increasingly conditions are attached to probation orders. Most recently, courts have gained the power to make drug-users undergo treatment and testing programmes, as well as to be subject to supervision by a probation officer.
- **Blurring**: formal social control no longer is confined to the prison but takes place in a variety of settings along the 'correctional continuum' such as probation hostels and day centres which are run by the Probation Service.
- **Penetration**: the combined effects of these tendencies are that the whole system of social control is now extending deeply into the informal networks of society.

Activity
How 'free' are you in the sense of 'not being governed by a law or regulation'? Brainstorm a list of all of the laws, formal and informal rules and regulations that you are subject to in the exercise of the daily life. Do you agree that we live in a controlled society?

A good illustration of Foucault's and Cohen's ideas in a contemporary context can be found in the work of **Shearing** and **Stenning** (1985). Their work highlights the changing nature of social control in the late twentieth century and is based on their analysis of Disney World. They note that the essential features of Disney's control system become apparent the moment the visitor enters Disney World. For example, visitors are told where to park, reminded to lock their cars and remember where they left them and then board the train which takes them to the park, taking care to follow safety procedures. Throughout the visit, customers are steered away from deviance and danger using monitoring devices that blend into the scenery. Based on this analysis they note the following points:

- Surveillance is increasingly being used for categories of people who might create opportunities for disorder.
- Control strategies are subtle, cooperative, and apparently non-coercive.
- Disney World is an excellent example of a private control system designed with the interests of business at heart.
- Surveillance is more concerned with the overt control of space than Foucault's notion.
- Technology is an important element of the control strategies used by Disney World.

The themes they highlight are increasingly important to crime prevention strategies in general.

Activity
If you have been to a concert or a sports event where a lot of people are present, think of all of the policing strategies that are used to prevent trouble occurring before and after the event. How are very large crowds controlled without the police or security groups making themselves too obvious?

PREVENTING CRIME

The different theoretical perspectives explored in Chapters 5 and 6 have different responses to the question: how should crime be prevented? Whilst some of the perspectives offer explanations of crime that can be translated in to crime prevention policies, other perspectives, particularly Marxist-inspired perspectives, argue that only fundamental social change can help to prevent crime. For these reasons, they have been branded as idealistic and have inspired the development of realist approaches to crime and crime control. Such approaches see crime as a problem and argue that we need to think realistically about what can be done about crime, avoiding utopian solutions. Realist approaches have been inspired by different political 'wings' and have contrasting views on the causes of crime and approaches to crime prevention.

LEFT REALISM AND SOCIAL CRIME PREVENTION

Left realism has two important elements to it:

1   It emphasises the social causes of crime, particularly relative deprivation (ie the perception that resources are distributed in an unfair manner) and political marginalisation.
2   It is concerned with the effects of crime on individuals such as victimisation and fear of crime, and also the effects on communities.

Whilst long-term goals of left realists include structural changes to promote social justice, left realists such as **Young** and **Matthews** (1992) support a variety of local immediate policies. These include:

* Promoting informal social control through families, schools and social services.
* Building strong communities, but as Young (1997, p 494) argues we should not 'expect them to resemble the soap operas we so avidly watch!'
* Multi-agency cooperation which is based on the view that the problem of crime can only be dealt with if agencies come together and cooperate.
* Work with victims in an attempt to minimise the harm suffered by crime victims.

Thus left realism combines a concern for victims with social crime prevention initiatives. These endeavour to address the root causes of crime and are focused primarily on deprived housing estates in high crime-rate areas. These projects involve active consultation with the local community in order to devise possible solutions to local problems. They are based on the concept of 'community safety' which regards crime prevention as not simply a matter for the police and encourages participation from all sections of society in the fight against crime. For example, neighbourhood support initiatives such as 'Safer Cities' programmes represent practical implementations of this type of thinking.

Activity
Talk to your local Community Police Officer and ask about crime prevention schemes operating in your local area. In your view, to what extent are they compatible with the ideas of left realism?

RIGHT REALISM AND SITUATIONAL CRIME PREVENTION

In contrast, right realism refers to a way of thinking about crime which is characterised primarily by a revived interest in individual processes as the causes of crime. Explanations of crime by right realists recognise the different factors that influence criminal behaviour including biological and psychological factors, but also recognise that individuals choose to commit crime.

US right realists have controversially suggested that crime is caused by wickedness (Wilson 1975) or illegitimacy (Murray 1990). In Britain, researchers particularly **Clarke** (1980), who can be loosely associated with this tradition, have advocated that offenders are rational, reasoning and normal rather than pathological. Consequently, crime is best understood as rational action performed by ordinary people acting under particular pressures and exposed to particular opportunities. Right realists advocate the use of **situational crime prevention** measures, which reduce opportunities for crime, and suggest this should be combined with criminal justice policies which aim to deter offenders. Situational crime prevention strategies aim to manage, design or manipulate the immediate environment in which crime occurs and thus are an example of an environment-focused crime prevention strategy (Walklate 1996).

Whilst the distinction between social and situational crime prevention is useful, **Walklate** (1996) provides a more detailed typology of crime prevention strategies, categorised in terms of focus. These are summarised in Table 14.

Table 14: *Typology of crime prevention strategies*

FOCUS ON CRIME PREVENTION STRATEGY	THEORETICAL BASE	EXAMPLES OF CRIME PREVENTION STRATEGIES
Offender-centred	The criminal justice system has a role to play in preventing further offending.	Harsh sentences to deter offenders from re-offending and encourage others not to offend. Treatment and rehabilitation programmes for offenders. Use of prison to incapacitate offenders for a specified period.
Victim-centred	Individuals have a role to play in preventing victimisation	Distribution of crime prevention literature advising individuals to take particular precautions. Insurance companies state that householders must take particular measures, eg fit specified locks.
Environment-centred	Opportunities for crime can be reduced.	More secure doors and windows (target hardening). Screening devices at airports (removing the means of criminal activity). CCTV (increase surveillance).
Community-centred	Crime prevention is not simply a matter for the police.	Neighbourhood Watch. Safter Cities programmes (eg involving partnerships with schools and local business).

Study point

Summarise the differences and similarities between left and right realism in terms of (a) causes of crime and (b) approaches to crime prevention.

CASE STUDY: CLOSED-CIRCUIT TELEVISION

The use of closed-circuit television (CCTV) in public and private places has burgeoned in the 1990s. **Beck** and **Willis** (1995) claim that £300 million a year is spent on CCTV and more than a million systems may be in use in Britain. The rapid expansion is showing no signs of slowing down. CCTV can now be found in the following places:

- **Public spaces**: CCTV initially developed in large cities but now the majority of cities and towns have installed sophisticated surveillance systems to watch public areas.
- **Commercial properties**: the origins of CCTV lie in the commercial sector with the use of these systems to enhance surveillance in properties such as department stores and shopping malls.

- **Public Buildings**: CCTV is increasingly used in public buildings such as hospitals and schools to monitor, in particular, individuals entering and exiting the building.
- **Residential areas**: less well-known is the use of CCTV in residential areas. CCTV systems are becoming increasingly affordable. There are examples of police surveillance systems in socially deprived areas. The first was set up in the West End of Newcastle in 1995. In the USA, where technologies are arguably at their most developed, CCTV is used particularly in affluent neighbourhoods and combined with other security measures such as private policing. Householders and Neighbourhood Watch groups in Britain are now purchasing CCTV systems.

Activity

List all the places where you are aware of closed-circuit television cameras in your local area.

Many companies, especially in the USA, sell clips from CCTV tapes to television companies to make comedy and documentary programmes. These can be seen on Cable TV stations but similar shows are also broadcast on British TV. How would you feel if your image was used in such a way?

A study conducted in Cambridge (Bennett and Gelsthorpe 1994) found that people had high expectations of what this technology could accomplish. Consequently, whilst they were aware of the potential drawbacks of CCTV and the implications for civil liberties, there was substantial public support for CCTV. What became evident from talking to people about their attitudes to CCTV (Emma Wincup, one of the authors of this text, was research assistant on this project) were the issues of effectiveness and civil liberties.

Points of evaluation

1 *The effectiveness of CCTV as a crime control strategy*

- Are offenders likely to be deterred from crime simply because they are aware that their actions might be caught on film?
- Does CCTV prevent crime or does it displace it to other places?
- Is it really a solution to the problem of crime, given that so much crime occurs in private spaces?
- If nothing else, can CCTV impact on fear of crime?

2 *The issue of civil liberties*

- What sorts of freedoms are given up as CCTV expands?
- Who should have the right to conduct surveillance?
- Who will watch over the watchers?

Study point
Consider the above questions on CCTV and make notes on your views.

SUMMARY

This chapter has explored the changing nature of crime control and social control from the nineteenth century onwards. We have explored how control mechanisms have penetrated deep into the social fabric of society. There has been a blurring of boundaries between the deviant and non-deviant and the public and the private. All of us are subject to perhaps greater social control than ever before, but as Shearing and Stenning (1985) suggest this is often so subtle that we may not realise we are being controlled. This fundamental change has far-reaching applications as the study of CCTV reveals.

Two important aspects of change in relation to crime control and social control as we approach the millennium are considered below:

1 There is an increased involvement of private companies in dealing with offenders and preventing crime. For example the development of private prisons (see Schichor 1995, Harding 1997), the introduction of electronic monitoring schemes (see Mair and Nee 1990, Mair and Mortimer 1996) and the provision of court escort services by private security companies such as Group Four (see Caddle 1995). Private companies have also been involved in the policing of commercial and residential areas (see Johnston 1992, Jones and Newburn 1998), and managing CCTV systems (see Norris et al 1998).
2 There is increased use of technology to control crime. New technologies to aid situational crime prevention are constantly being developed.

It is important to note that crime control and social control do not occur in a vacuum. Moreover, the process of controlling crime reflects, and reinforces, existing social divisions. As we noted in Chapter 4 and again in this chapter, the criminal justice system responds in different ways to different social groups. For example, research has suggested that police officers target particular groups such as young men or ethnic minorities.

Similarly the crime prevention literature (see Pease 1997 for an overview) suggests that the most vulnerable groups have the least access to particular situational crime prevention measures. As **Stanko** (1990) has noted, crime prevention advice has particular implications for women. Advising women to modify their behaviour restricts their lives and perpetuates the myth of the 'safe' home and the 'dangerous' streets.

STUDY GUIDES

Key Concept Activity

Make a key concept card for each of the following terms:

- formal social control
- informal social control
- criminal justice
- realism (left and right)
- crime prevention (social and situational).

Group Work

1 As a group, identify and recognise all of the features of social control that are evident within your organisation. If you are in a school for instance, how do the staff control assemblies? Generally, few pupils really enjoy them or want to be present. Look at both formal and informal sanctions that may be used to ensure that pupils behave in a manner that the staff consider appropriate.

2 Organise a formal debate on one of the following propositions:

- *'The reintroduction of hanging for a wider range of offences in this country would help to reduce the murder rate.'*
  You will need to gather data on the number of murders and on the arguments that are used both for and against capital punishment.
- *'CCTV is an effective crime prevention strategy.'*
  Again, you will need to research the effectiveness of CCTV through reading relevant research studies and contacting the police and other agencies to request statistics.

3 Gather data from a variety of respondents and pool your results. Find out what attitudes people have towards the proposition that the police should be armed with handguns to prevent crime. Here you will need to gather comparative data on the crime rates of a variety of countries and to consider the historical reasons why the British police are not armed while in other countries they are armed. You will have to consider what general position people around you seem to hold and to see if you can equate their views with sociological perspectives. You might find that your pooled results and discussion would make a good wall display. To develop the work, you could then ask members of the police force to consider their views on the issue.

The material in this chapter offers fertile ground for coursework projects because there is so much to consider in terms of public attitudes to crime and crime prevention. We are no longer considering the question of why crime occurs, but have redirected academic attention towards the question of crime control and prevention. Practical and ethical considerations, which should be at the forefront of your thinking when looking at personal motivation, become much less significant in terms of the formulation of the investigations into social attitude formation.

Attitude surveys into elements of social control offer by far the simplest area for discussion in coursework in the study of crime and deviance. Your questionnaire designs will have to be extremely careful, as you may find that in an attitude survey, a particular danger is that a badly designed question will introduce considerable bias into your results. Make sure that you pilot this type of work carefully.

1 *'A qualitative study into experience of jury service'*

Use a snowball sample of self-referring respondents who have all experienced jury service in recent years. (A snowball sample is built up through informants. You begin with one respondent and ask them to introduce you to others.) You are certain to find a small number of people on the staff of your college and amongst your immediate acquaintances. Interview these people about their experiences of being on a jury. Keep your sample small and ensure that your interview schedule is detailed. Shallow questioning may mean that you cannot develop a full critical analysis of the issues you are studying.

Ask whether the sample agreed with the decisions made by the rest of the jury. Did they have reservations about the process? What were the other jurors like? Did they take the experience seriously? You might need to consider whether the jury came from a different social mix from the defendants, though this may not be something that your sample will have noted at the time. You will have to read between the lines of what is said in order to understand some of the concerns that members of the public have about process of trial by jury. This means that you will have to record and transcribe interviews carefully.

2 *'How much knowledge do people actually have of how the law operates in practice?'*

Select a variety of crimes of various types including controversial ones such as child abuse and drink driving. Using a simple quantitative questionnaire design, ask a variety of people such as those shopping on a Saturday what they think the most appropriate punishment in law should be for those found guilty. Ask them why. Your sample should be very wide. You will need to do a little research to discover what the sentences and punishments for your selection of crimes actually are in practice. You could develop this work by also asking them what they think the usual or average sentences are for different crimes.

The content of this chapter is highly significant in terms of the practical application of the theoretical understandings that have been discussed on earlier chapters. You must show that you are aware of current developments in your answers. Sociology is an organic subject which constantly grows and develops, and where theory underlies current social administration and practice.

You have been advised frequently in this text to be certain that you are aware of current events by reading newspapers and watching documentaries. You will be rewarded in the examination for including contemporary examples to illustrate theoretical ideas.

Evaluate the evidence to suggest that social control is becoming embedded 'deep into the fabric of our society'.

This question is asking you to consider a number of issues and you will have to address all of them to offer a good overview of the debate:

1 You will have to define the nature of social control and to do this you ought really consider what each of the perspectives has to offer in terms of a definition.
2 The next part of the question requires that you consider the phrase in quotation marks. You will need to identify this correctly as a view that is linked to the work of Foucault and developed by theorists such as Cohen, and you will have to explain this idea.
3 The body of the answer will have to address the question of whether or not you feel that social control is embedded deeply into the fabric of our society. There are three possible positions: you agree, you disagree, or you feel that there is an equally good argument both for and against. In this case, the simplest position to take is one of agreement and you will need to provide examples of social control, which you have gleaned from the whole chapter.

9

CRIME, DEVIANCE AND SOCIAL CONTROL: KEY THEMES AND CONTEMPORARY DEBATES

Introduction

IN THIS FINAL chapter, we pause briefly to reflect critically on the study of crime, deviance and social control before moving on to examine contemporary theoretical and policy debates. The aim of this chapter is not to offer a summary of earlier discussions, rather to consolidate your understanding of key themes relevant to the study of crime, deviance and social control; and to emphasise contemporary concerns amongst criminologists and policy makers. This will be useful preparation for the examination, particularly if you practice the general questions which require you to have an overview of the subject.

We will end by providing guidance on examination and revision technique. However, the aim of this chapter, or indeed this book, is not simply to prepare you for the examination but to encourage you to engage with ongoing debates about crime and to consider whether crime can be explained. We hope we have inspired some readers to develop their interests through related coursework projects and further study. Finally, the study guide section of this chapter is rather more detailed than in many previous chapters. If you choose to produce a piece of research for examination based on the study of crime and deviance, then you are well advised to read this section before you begin your study to avoid possible pitfalls for the inexperienced.

Table 15: *Key concepts and debates raised in this chapter*	
KEY DEBATES	KEY ISSUES RAISED
1 *Theoretical Debates*	
• Feminism	• Is criminology a gendered discipline?
• Modernism and postmodernism	• Can criminologists study crime and think of ways to eradicate it?
• Realism	• Crime is a problem which needs to be responded to.
• Administrative criminology	• Should we abandon the search for the causes of crime?
2 *Policy Debates*	
• The 'New' Left	• Society needs to be tough on crime and tough on the causes of crime.
• The 'New' Right	• Punitive approaches are needed to deter offenders.

KEY CONCEPTS AND DEBATES IN THIS CHAPTER

KEY CONCEPTS

- crime
- deviance
- social order
- social control
- social dimensions of crime, deviance and social control (gender, ethnicity, age and social class)
- social geography.

KEY THEMES REVISITED

KEY THEORETICAL CONCEPTS

Your study so far should have made clear that definitions of crime are subject to dispute. Although criminologists cannot agree on a definition of crime, they agree that crime is a contested concept. For some theorists, the lack of agreement on the appropriate use of term 'crime' leads them to suggest that the term should be discarded altogether. **Hulsman** (1986) and **De Haan** (1991) advocate this position. They argue that alternative terms should be used such as 'social harm' or 'injury'. Different views as to how crime should be conceived are also the subject of public debate that may come to influence political decisions concerning policies connected with crime. Deviance is even more problematic to define than crime because it can include such a wide range of behaviours. Thus debates about what constitutes crime and deviance are not merely academic ones but political and popular ones.

In Chapter 2, we drew your attention to the problem of defining crime in terms of a violation of the criminal law. We noted the need to explore the ways in which behaviours are criminalised and the process of labelling individuals as criminals; in other words to analyse the social construction of crime and criminals. We observed the differing definitions of crime held by the main theoretical perspectives. The lack of consensus on what constitutes crime is not surprising. Criminology, like sociology, is characterised by a wide variety of theoretical perspectives. Each of these offers different views of how society is organised and how social order is maintained. Their conception of crime reflects this. Social order is itself a contested concept. We can compare and contrast the different visions of society held by functionalists, Marxists, interactionists and feminists. Despite the different views of the social order, crime is often viewed as the major threat to social order and thus it needs to be controlled. The work of Durkheim is perhaps an exception here.

Activity
Revise the theoretical perspectives discussed in this text, making note of both the differences and the similarities between each set of theories. Summarise this as a set of points of agreement and disagreement. You should refer to the key concepts summary table at the beginning of this chapter to help you focus your work.

Crime control refers to organised responses to crime which generally focus on dealing with offenders through the criminal justice system. Increasingly the criminal justice system is placing greater emphasis on the needs and rights of victims (Zedner 1997). Crime control can be approached by employing one of two alternative strategies; one emphasising punishment, the other rehabilitation. Most recently, punitive approaches to deal with offenders have been prioritised. Crime control also relates to the *prevention* of particular crimes. The study of crime prevention strategies illustrates how the boundaries with social control overlap and are blurred. Social control refers to the overall means by which social conformity and regulation are secured and this affects all members of society not just criminals.

SOCIAL DIMENSIONS OF CRIME, DEVIANCE AND SOCIAL CONTROL

Throughout this text we have highlighted the need to analyse the social dimensions of crime, deviance and social control. In particular, we have argued that the study of crime and deviance needs to consider issues of gender, ethnicity, age and social class. These social divisions are central to our understanding of:

1 patterns of offending
2 patterns of actual victimisation and fear of victimisation
3 the administration of social control and crime control.

Activity

Copy the following table into your notes and attempt to complete it. In order to do so, you will need to critically evaluate the research evidence discussed in this book.

SOCIAL DIMENSION	LEVELS OF OFFENDING BEHAVIOUR	LEVELS OF VICTIMISATION	LEVELS OF FEAR OF CRIME	CRIMINAL JUSTICE RESPONSES
Age	High among the young, lower among the old.			
Gender			Higher among women, lower for men.	
Ethnicity				Evidence of discrimination against Afro–Caribbeans.
Class		Working classes experience greater victimisation.		

In Chapters 3 and 4, we explored the methodological problems associated with exploring patterns of offending and victimisation. Nevertheless, we can conclude that young, lower-class males commit a disproportionate amount of crime. Once we take hidden crime into account, women, ethnic minorities and the poor experience a disproportionate amount of victimisation. One of the main problems facing a researcher who wishes to explore the relationship between social divisions and patterns of offending and victimisation is that often the data is produced by agencies of crime control. These agencies do not operate in a vacuum. Particular social groups are likely to be subject to greater control than others. For example, gender differences in terms of levels of offending are likely to be influenced by the following factors:

- The greater social control of women (explaining why women do not offend).
- The targetting of males by agents of crime control such as the police (explaining why men are more likely to be caught offending).

We live in a very diverse society. There are other social divisions other than those we have highlighted that are important to the study of crime and deviance. For example, we could also explore issues of sexuality. Research has high-lighted the disproportionate victimisation experienced by homosexuals (Herek and Berrill 1992).

We have also suggested the need for an analysis of locality and community. Criminology can be viewed as an interdisciplinary 'meeting place' (McLaughlin and Muncie 1998). The ideas of social geography have had a considerable influence on our understanding of crime, particularly urban crime. We can trace this back to the work of the Chicago School discussed in Chapter 4 which argued that crime and deviance can be viewed as a product of social disorganisation. As we noted in Chapter 3, levels of victimisation and fear are greater amongst those who live in cities. The city, or at least particular areas within it (see Chapter 4), is often constructed as a 'dangerous' place (Graham and Clarke 1996).

The notion that crime can be mapped spatially is central to contemporary crime prevention policy. A number of initiatives have been introduced to improve the quality of city life and reduce crime, for instance, the Safer Cities Programme launched in 1988. Many of the situational crime prevention initiatives discussed in Chapter 8, such as CCTV, are directed towards particular areas such as city centres. The police have also developed area-based policing strategies concentrating on areas where crime is greatest (McLaughlin 1996b).

Study point
Why might the patrolling of city centres and the use of CCTV increase the proportion of young males who appear in offending statistics?

CONTEMPORARY THEORETICAL DEBATES

THE IMPACT OF FEMINIST PERSPECTIVES

The impact of feminist perspectives on criminology is discussed in detail in Chapter 6. Feminist perspectives have attracted critical comment but they have been very influential. As **Gelsthorpe** (1997) argues, feminists have done much to question masculinist viewpoints of criminology, and to alter thinking. There now appears to be a convergence of interests between feminism and criminology in some quarters, and thus scope for positive dialogue. It is worth re-emphasising that there is a growing body of theoretical and empirical work being done on men and masculinity and its relationship with crime. Crucially, this has broadened the concern with gender and crime, which traditionally focused on women and crime, and led to more criminological researchers developing an interest in gender issues. Despite its traditional focus on men who offend, until recently criminology had only studied this group as examples of *offenders* rather than *men* who offend.

Debates within feminism and feminist criminology have been in part responsible for the beginnings of a postmodern critique of criminology, initially and notably advanced by **Carol Smart** (1990).

Activity
Consolidate your understanding of this debate by suggesting differences between 'malestream' and 'feminist' criminology.

DEBATES ABOUT MODERNISM AND POSTMODERNISM

Modernism often means different things to different people but in the context of the debate about modernism and postmodernism, it has a specific meaning:

- **Modernism**: modernism here refers to particular ways of thinking about the world which have their origin in the enlightenment of the seventeenth and eighteenth centuries (Brown 1996). In this sense, both sociology and criminology can be considered modernist projects. Criminological theories are wedded to the modernist principle that knowledge about crime can be deployed to solve the problem of crime.
- **Postmodernism**: postmodernists challenge and reject modernist conceptions of the social world, of knowledge about it, and of the pursuit of progress and better futures (Bilton et al 1996). They reject all-encompassing theories of human life, which offer a vision of social progress. These are termed 'grand' or 'meta' narratives and an example of such a modernist narrative is Marxism. Postmodernist theories do not themselves constitute one view, but represent a variety of positions that have in common a sense that society is 'relativist'. They claim that for most people there is not an objective 'thing' known as good or bad, truth or lies. Postmodernism is essentially very critical of Marxist theorising. Society, according to postmodernists, is not a march of progress, but is an individualistic and consumer-based creation. People no longer rely on old certainties and cannot draw on their communities for a sense of identity or self.

The debate between modernism and postmodernism is primarily a debate about the nature of culture and society itself. Its impact on criminology has been limited and it has more impact on other sociological debates, for instance sociology of the media debates. It is, however, a discussion that is of increasing importance in academic texts and one which you should show some familiarity with in examinations.

Postmodernists have argued that criminology tends to impose some essential unity and totality on the study of crime, categorising a vast range of activities as criminal. Criminology also assumes general theories of crime can be made and solutions offered. As we discussed in Chapter 2, crime is a contested concept and we can argue that, without this unity, the discipline of criminology is undermined.

In sum, postmodernists have questioned the viability of criminology's traditional modernist orientation based on a commitment to applying reliable knowledge and theorising to construct solutions to the crime problem (Bilton et al 1996). The implications for the discipline of criminology are great. Rather than simply focusing on explanations of crime, criminology is expanding its focus and developing new concerns about crime issues such as fear of crime, victims of crime and media representations. However, many criminologists remain sceptical about the postmodernist critique and adopt a realist approach.

Study point

What difficulties would someone have if they attempted to apply a postmodernist analysis to the study of criminal behaviour?

THE DEVELOPMENT OF REALIST APPROACHES

The 1980s witnessed the growth of realist approaches to crime by those of different political persuasions as a response to radical criminological perspectives (see Chapter 5). Left realism has been discussed in this text in Chapter 3 in relation to work on victim surveys and fear of crime. Both left and right realism are explored in Chapter 8 and their respective crime prevention strategies compared and contrasted. Both left and right realism have been influential in shaping policy debates.

Whilst left and right realism are clearly distinct strands of realist approaches, we can identify points of convergence. **Young** (1994) argues that these include the following:

1　Both see crime as a real problem.
2　Both suggest that crime control strategies need to be altered.
3　Both are realistic about what can be done about crime.
4　Both emphasise the need for closely monitored research and intervention.

Study point

Evaluate which contemporary perspective on crime you find most satisfactory, postmodernism or realism. Expect your notes to be short initially, but return to the exercise until your understanding of the two positions is clearer.

THE GROWTH OF ADMINISTRATIVE CRIMINOLOGY

Young (1986) suggests criminology faced a crisis at the end of the 1960s. Crime rates continued to rise despite the creation of a more affluent society and a more developed system of crime control. As a consequence, both classical and positivist ideas were fundamentally challenged.

Whilst some criminologists responded to this by pursuing radical or critical agendas, others followed a different path which Young terms 'administrative criminology'. The basic tenets of this include (Jupp 1996):

- a lack of concern with the causes of crime
- a belief that free will underlies criminal actions
- an emphasis on policies to prevent and deter crime.

Administrative criminology adheres to the view that the causes of crime cannot be identified with any certainty and thus it is futile to tackle such causes in order to reduce crime rates. Consequently, they suggest the emphasis should be on strategies and policies to deter the rational actor from committing criminal acts.

The tenets of administrative criminology are very close to those associated with right realists. In Britain, the work of **Clarke** (discussed in Chapter 8), a leading Home Office researcher in the 1980s, was particularly influential. The research agenda was typically organised around the examination of issues such as situational factors, evaluation of situational crime prevention strategies and patterns of victimisation. Much of this work has been conducted, or funded, by the Home Office.

Study point

Can crime be considered the work of rational actors? List points both for and against this view with particular reference to the following crimes: rape, car theft, burglary, arson, child abuse by family members and drug abuse.

CONTEMPORARY POLICY DEBATES

THE 'NEW' RIGHT

The shift to the right politically in Britain from 1979 (the beginning of the Thatcher 'era') had major implications for criminal justice policy. Law and order emerged as a key issue which was fuelled by, and fed off, growing concerns and fears about crime. The emphasis of Thatcherism was on individuals rather than society. Applied to crime control, situational crime prevention measures were favoured, as was an increasingly punitive approach to offenders. New legislation and policies were introduced to increase police powers and allow the courts to give tougher sentences to offenders. The aim of this approach was to deter would-be offenders. This punitive approach was accelerated from 1993 when Michael Howard became Home Secretary. He is best known for his 'Prison Works' strategy that led to a rising prison population which has yet to be halted.

Activity

List arguments for and against the use of prison as a strategy for society to deal with crime. Consider the following issues: retribution, deterrence, protection of society and rehabilitation.

THE 'NEW' LEFT

Traditionally, those on the left have advocated a welfare approach to dealing with offenders, emphasising the need to rehabilitate offenders. In addition, they have stressed the utility of social crime prevention policies. The Labour Government elected on 1 May 1997 adopted a somewhat different position and summed up its position in the slogan 'tough on crime, tough on the causes of crime'. There was no reversal of existing legislation which favoured punitive approaches, and this was reinforced in many ways through agreement to a programme of prison building (with private finance). At the time of writing, major new legislation has come onto the statute books but the results have yet to be seen. Two key elements of the Crime and Disorder Act 1998 are (see National Association for the Care and Resettlement of Offenders 1998):

1 Local authorities and the police will have to draw up crime and disorder reduction strategies in their areas, cooperating with the probation and health authorities.

2 A wide range of new orders will be introduced to deal with specific crime problems: anti-social behaviour orders to be applied against those who alarm, distress or harass; sex offender orders; parenting orders; child safety orders and child curfew orders.

The Labour Government has also created a Social Exclusion Unit. Part of its work has been to tackle the problems of the poorest neighbourhoods, including crime. Additionally, an extra £250 million will be made available between 1998 and 2001 for crime reduction projects which will then be evaluated.

Activity

Read the following paragraph which draws conclusions from a description of a research project.

> The best way to minimise the harmful effects of maternal incarceration for children is to reduce the number of women going to prison. Given that the majority of females in prisons are there for theft and other property offences, the use of prison for many of these women is questionable. An increased use of community penalties with the type of programme (used) for drug offenders if adequately resourced would also help to reduce the risk of the children of women in prison becoming the next generation of inmates. But if such programmes are to be successful, they must also go hand in hand with getting tough on the causes of crime including issues of poverty and abuse.
>
> Jane Woodrow *The Guardian* 11 November 1998

1 Identify the sociological perspective(s) that may have informed the research design.
2 Identify the sociological perspective(s) that informs the conclusion.
3 Suggest ideas for programmes that would rehabilitate female offenders so that they did not re-offend using ideas based on left realism.
4 How might those working in the right-realist tradition suggest that the problem of female offenders should be dealt with?
5 What effect do you think that the new legislation suggested by the Labour Government may have on the number of females in prison?

SUMMARY

Debates about crime, and how best to control it, are ongoing. In this chapter we have explored some of the issues likely to frame the future of the study of crime, deviance and social control. At a theoretical level, some major challenges to the discipline are taking place and the future is likely to be marked by theoretical diversity and, perhaps, fragmentation. At a political level, issues of law and order are receiving unprecedented attention. Pessimistically, we could point to our perceived inability to explain crime and offer solutions to the problem of crime. More optimistically, we emphasise the need for criminologists to engage in theoretical debates and to continue to conduct research on a diversity of criminological topics.

Key Concept Activity

At this point, it might be as well to consolidate and develop your understanding of the sociology of crime and deviance in the following ways:

1 Return to the various chapters of the book and mark areas that you find interesting or difficult so that you can speak to your teacher. Do not expect to have learned a great deal on a first reading; concentrate on understanding the broader picture.
2 Return to the various exercises and discussion points. Attempt them again and see whether your answers to them have changed substantially now that your understanding of the topic has grown.
3 Read around your subject in other books and journals. *Sociology Review* or *S: The Sociology Magazine* are highly recommended. There are other books and materials available to develop your knowledge and suggestions are included at the end of the book. You may find revision texts useful although they sometimes lack the necessary depth. Your study folder should take on the appearance of a scrapbook with ideas, notes and cuttings developing the key ideas.

Coursework

Crime and criminal behaviour may seem exciting to study and many students are attracted to these topics. However, you are advised to plan research into criminality with caution because there are serious ethical and practical problems for the unwary. Listen carefully to the advice that you are offered by your lecturer or teacher and take notes; the objections and difficulties raised should provide a basis for the context and the evaluation sections of your coursework. If you teacher is doubtful about your choice of topic then take it as a bad sign and think again.

Prior to commencing your study, there are a number of practical issues to consider. These include time and resources but you should also think carefully when designing a study about how you will analyse the data you collect. You may find numerical data is easier to process for coursework purposes. After considering these issues, you may decide to use secondary data. Research into crime using secondary data obtained from a variety of sources can be relatively straightforward and very interesting to undertake. There are enormous amounts of data available. However, crime statistics are notoriously unreliable in certain areas and you should check Chapter 5 of this text carefully because statistics gathered by other agencies may not tell you what you want or need to know. Sources could include data obtained from your local police force, government statistics such as *Social Trends* and cross-cultural data (available on the Internet).

Studies into drugs, under-age drinking and under-age sex are over-popular and often badly done. It would be difficult to show any real originality using these themes and, unless the ethics of the research design are fully explored in the context and methods sections, the work will not score well in the marking. However, if you are interested in deviance then consider rule-breaking which is of less moral and social significance than law-breaking. Those of you studying in schools may consider the impact of school rule-breaking, such as truancy. Colleges may have a more relaxed regime, but careful thought may offer you an example of institutional rule-breaking and student unconformity. Those with jobs can examine how rules are applied in the workplace. The use and enforcement of dress and jewellery codes, smoking rules and timekeeping in any institution will provide classic examples for interesting studies.

Summary of issues

- Keep your coursework design simple. The emphasis is not on what you discover but the methods that you use.
- Take your teacher's advice. He or she is the expert and will see problems that you will not be aware of.
- Read widely before making a final decision as to the exact wording of your title to the methodology that you will use.
- Do not undertake work that may be unethical or impractical.

You may find that, if you are having trouble identifying a suitable topic, many of the activities listed in the various chapters offer a starting point for adaptation.

Revision Hints

- Make sure your notes are clear, systematic and well spaced out on the page.
- You are advised to create contents lists for your folders.
- Read and reread your notes on a regular basis.
- Write down the key facts in pen and your own evaluations and commentary on the notes in pencil.
- If a study is relevant to more than one substantive area, photocopy notes for both section of your folder.
- Share your work as much as possible with other people. Compare essays and discuss your ideas in your own time.
- Keep a vocabulary notebook for your own use. Write down unfamiliar words and their meanings and check them regularly.

Exam Hints

Find out as much as you can about the syllabus and the assessment criteria for the examinations by writing to the examining board. Purchase copies of past papers to give you a guide as to the style and format for the questions.

Refer back to Chapter 1 for general advice on tackling exam questions.

Practice Questions

Refer to your notes for each of the different chapters of this book and practise the following questions:

1 Evaluate the contribution of Marxist sociology to an understanding of social control in our society.
2 Assess the view that deviance is functional for our society.
3 To what extent can it be argued that criminal behaviour is normal behaviour?
4 Is crime a masculine activity?
5 Evaluate the suggestion that a rise in crime statistics is proof of a rise in crime itself.
6 Can law enforcement agencies and the criminal justice system be said to create criminal behaviour?
7 What understandings do sub-cultural theories bring to the study of crime?
8 'Crime occurs in all social classes but the enforcement of criminal laws and the types of crime committed vary significantly between social classes.' Discuss.
9 Is there a relationship between the mass media, social control and crime?

FURTHER READING

Defining Crime and Deviance

Griffin, C. and Willmott, S. (1998) 'Who are the criminals?', *Sociology Review*,
    September, 23–26.
This article draws on recent research with male offenders and explores their
definitions of crime and their distinction between acceptable crimes (eg social
security fraud, economic crimes to provide for their children and wives) and
unacceptable crimes (eg sexual offences, 'mugging' old ladies).

Knelman, J. (1998) 'Women Murderers in Victorian Britain', *History Today*,
    August, 9–14.
This article discusses the social construction of female murderers in Victorian
Britain and develops many of the issues discussed in this chapter from a
historical and media studies perspective.

Muncie, J. and McLaughlin, E. (1996) (eds.) *The Problem of Crime*, London: Sage.
This edited collection provides a detailed discussion of definitions of crime, the
history of crime and many examples of hidden crime.

Measuring Crime

Coleman, C. and Moynihan, J. (1996) *Understanding Crime Data: Haunted by the Dark
    Figure*, Buckingham: Open University Press.
This is a clear and practical text which offers a detailed discussion of the different
sources of crime data.

Social Trends, London: HMSO.
This official publication dedicates a chapter to crime and justice and offers a user-
friendly introduction to crime data. It is available in public libraries and on
CD-Rom.

Walklate, S. (1994) 'Crime Victims: Another 'Ology'?', *Sociology Review*, February,
    29–33.
Walklate discusses a growing concern amongst criminologists with the victims of
crime and reviews available data on victimisation.

Williams, J. (1998) 'Research Roundup: Crime Trends and Fear of Crime', *Sociology
    Review*, April 6–8.
This short article offers a summary of recent research.

Patterns of Crime and Criminal Behaviour

Coleman, C. and Moynihan, J. (1996) *Understanding Crime Data: Haunted by the
    Dark Figure*, Buckingham: Open University Press.
This is a very accessible text which explores what different data sources tell us
about patterns of crime and criminal behaviour.

Croall, H. (1998) *Crime and Society*, London: Longman.
This introductory text explains how crime can be related to social inequality in society and explores the patterning of different types of crime.

Explaining Crime and Deviance: The Development of Sociological Approaches

Many of the texts written on theories of crime and criminal behaviour are hard-going but the following are recommended:

Croall, H. (1998) *Crime and Society*, London: Longman.
Chapter 3 explores structural and cultural explanations of crime.

Heidensohn, F. (1995) *Women and Crime*, London: Macmillan.
This text offers an account of the misrepresentation (and often neglect) of female offenders in individual and social explanations of criminal behaviour.

Muncie, J., McLaughlin, E. and Langan, M. (1996) (eds.) *Criminological Perspectives*, London: Sage.
This edited collection contains short abridged extracts of original work by many of the theorists referred to in this chapter.

Explaining Crime and Deviance: The Growth of Radical Approaches

Croall, H. (1998) *Crime and Society*, London: Longman.
Chapter 4 offers a discussion of criminological approaches from labelling theory to realist criminology. Chapter 8 has a summary of the development of feminist perspectives.

Heidensohn, F. (1989) *Crime and Society*, London: Macmillan.
This text includes a chapter entitled 'Changing Perspectives on Crime: From Interactionism to Critical Criminology'.

Muncie, J., McLaughlin, E. and Langan, M. (1996) (eds.) *Criminological Perspectives*, London: Sage.
This edited collection contains short abridged extracts of original work by many of the theorists referred to in this chapter.

Suicide: The Ultimate Deviance

Giddens, A. (1978) *Durkheim*, London: Fontana.
A useful and concise introduction to the different works of Durkheim with a critical commentary at the end of the book.

Jones, M. (1998) 'Suicide Revisited', *Sociology Review*, September, 32–3.
A short article which explores the suicides of members of the cult, Heaven's Gate, and Michael Hutchence and tries to fit these within a Durkheim framework.

Taylor, S. (1988) *Suicide*, London: Longman.
A short book providing an overview of the sociology of suicide, sociological explanations of suicide and suicide research.

CONTROLLING CRIME

Davies, M. Croall, H. and Tryer, J. (1998) (eds.) *Criminal Justice*, London: Longman.
This introductory text provides a detailed account of the working of the criminal justice system in England and Wales.

McLaughlin, E. and Muncie, J. (1996) (eds.) *Controlling Crime*, London: Sage.
This text offers a comprehensive discussion of the origins of agencies of crime control and contemporary debates about ways to deal with the problem of crime. It is particularly useful because it highlights issues of race and gender which are often neglected.

Muncie, J. McLaughlin, E. and Langan, M. (1996) (eds.) *Criminological Perspectives*, London: Sage.
This edited collection contains short abridged extracts of original work by many of the theorists referred to in this chapter including Foucault, Clarke, and Shearinag and Stenning.

Newburn, T. (1995) *Crime and Criminal Justice Policy*, London: Macmillan.
This text is designed as an introduction to the recent history of criminal justice policy, broadly defined to include the courts, the probation service, prisons, the police, as well as work with victims. However, a lot of attention is paid to longer-term historical transformations. This is one of the most readable texts on criminal justice but note that criminal justice policy is changing rapidly and therefore this text, or indeed any other, will not be fully up-to-date.

CRIME, DEVIANCE AND SOCIAL CONTROL: KEY THEMES AND CONTEMPORARY DEBATES

Brown, P. (1996) 'Modernism. Post-modernism and Sociological Theory: A Beginner's Guide', *Sociology Review*, February 22–25.
A short article which explains clearly the significance of debates about modernism and postmodernism for sociological theory. It includes suggestions as to how students can apply these debates to A Level examination questions.

Walklate, S. (1998) *Understanding Criminology*, Buckingham: Open University Press.
Described as a critical overview of the criminological enterprise over the past 20 years, this text provides a useful discussion of criminological theory and its relationship with social policy and political concerns.

Criminal Justice Matters (Winter 1998/1999)
This edition is entitled *Criminology and its Uses* is dedicated to articles on debates within the criminological enterprise around theory and their implications for criminal justice policy.

ADDITIONAL RESOURCES

USEFUL ADDRESSES

The following voluntary organisations produce a wide range of materials on criminological and criminal justice issues including fact sheets and magazines:

Institute for the Study and Treatment of Delinquency (ISTD)
Centre for Crime and Justice Studies
Kings College London
8th Floor
75–79 York Road
London
SE1 7AW

National Association for the Care and Resettlement of Offenders (NACRO)
169 Clapham Road
London
SW9 0PU

Prison Reform Trust
15 Northburgh Street
London
EC1V 0AH

The Howard League for Penal Reform
708 Holloway Road
London
N19 3NL

The Home Office produce statistical bulletins and reports of research findings; many of which are free upon request from *Home Office*, 50 Queen Anne's Gate, London, SW1H 9AT.

JOURNALS

- *British Criminology Conferences: Selected Proceedings* (free on-line journal) http://www.lboro.ac.uk/departments/ss/bsc/bsccp/index.html
- *British Journal of Criminology* (academic journal)
- *Criminal Justice Matters* (produced by ISTD)
- *The Howard Journal of Criminal Justice* (academic journal)
- *Sociology Review* (Aimed at those studying sociology for the first time.)

WEB SITES

- The Association for the Teaching of Social Sciences: http://www.le.ac.uk/education/centres/ATSS/atss.html
- The Home Office Web site provides criminal justice statistics, details of criminal justice policies and a list of all the publications available: http://www.homeoffice.gov.uk
- ISTD: http://www.kcl.ac.uk.orgs.istd
- Cardiff University: (a) Introduction to Sociology Web site: http://www.cf.ac.uk/uwcc/socas/ugyear1/introsoc/index.html
  (b) Selected Criminology Resources Web site: http:www.cf.ac.uk.infos/information/crimweb.html

BIBLIOGRAPHY

Abercrombie, N., Warde, A., Soothill, K., Urry, J. and Walby, S. (1994) (2nd ed.) *Contemporary British Society*, Cambridge: Polity Press.

Adler, F. (1975) *Sisters in Crime*, New York: McGraw-Hill.

Allen, H. (1987) *Justice Unbalanced*, Buckingham: Open University Press.

Atkinson, J. (1978) *Discovering Suicide*, London: Macmillan.

Baldwin, J. and Bottoms, A. (1976) *The Urban Criminal*, London: Tavistock.

Barclay, G. (1995) (ed.) *Digest 3: Information on the Criminal Justice System in England and Wales*, London: HMSO.

Beccaria, C. (1764) 'On Crimes and Punishment', extract reprinted in J. Muncie, E. McLaughlin and M. Langan (1996) (eds.) *Criminological Perspectives*, London: Sage.

Beck, A. and Willis, A. (1995) *Crime and Security*, Leicester: Perpetuity Press.

Becker, H. (1963) *Outsiders*, New York: Free Press.

Bennet, T. and Gelsthorpe, L. (1994) *Public Attitudes to CCTV*, report to Cambridge Council Safer Cambridge Group.

Bilton, T., Bonnett, K., Jones, P., Stanworth, M., Sheard, K. and Webster, A. (1987) (2nd ed.) *Introductory Sociology*, London: Macmillan.

Bilton, T., Bonnett, K., Jones, P., Stanworth, M., Sheard, K. and Webster A. (1996) (3rd ed.) *Introductory Sociology*, London: Macmillan.

Bonger, W. (1916) 'Criminality and Economic Conditions', extract reprinted in J. Muncie, E. McLaughlin and M. Langan (1996) (eds.) *Criminological Perspectives*, London: Sage.

Bottom, A. and Wiles, P. (1997) 'Environmental Criminology' in M. Maguire, R. Morgan and R. Reiner (eds.) (2nd ed.) *The Oxford Handbook of Criminology*, Oxford: Oxford University Press.

Box. S. (1983) *Power, Crime and Mystification*, London: Tavistock.

Brown, I. and Hullin, R. (1992) 'A Study of Sentencing in Leeds Magistrates' Courts: The Treatment of Ethnic Minority and White Offenders', *British Journal of Criminology*, 32: 41–53.

Brown, P. (1996) 'Modernism, Post-modernism and Sociological Theory: A Beginner's Guide', *Sociology Review*, February 22–25.

Caddle, D. (1995) *A Survey of the Prisoner Escort and Custody Service Provided by Group 4 and by Securicor Custodial Services*, London: HMSO.

Campbell, A. (1984) *The Girls in the Gang*, Oxford: Basil Blackwell.

Carlen, P. (1983) *Women's Imprisonment*, London: Routledge.

Carlen, P. (1988) *Women, Crime and Poverty*, Buckingham: Open University Press.

Carlen, P. (1998) *Sledgehammer: Women's Imprisonment at the Millennium*, London: Macmillan.

Chadwick, K. and Little, C. (1987) 'The Criminalisation of Women' in P. Scraton (ed.) *Law, Order and the Authoritarian State*, Buckingham: Open University Press.

Chambliss, W. (1975) 'Towards a Political Economy of Crime', *Theory and Society*, 2: 149–70.

Clarke, R. (1980) 'Situational Crime Prevention: Theory and Practice', *British Journal of Criminology*, 20: 136–47.

Cloward, R. and Ohlin, L. (1960) *Delinquency and Opportunity*, New York: Free Press.

Cohen, A. (1955) *Delinquent Boys*, London: Free Press.

Cohen, A. and Short, J. (1958) 'Research in Delinquent Subcultures', *Journal of Social Issues*, 14: 20–37.

Cohen, S. (1973) *Folk Devils and Moral Panics*, London: Paladin.

Cohen, S. (1985) *Visions of Social Control*, Cambridge: Polity Press.

Cohen, S. (1993) 'Human Rights and Crimes of the State: The Culture of Denial', *Australian and New Zealand Journal of Criminology*, 26: 87–115.

Coleman, C. and Moynihan, J. (1996) *Understanding Crime Data*, Buckingham: Open University Press.

Cook, D. (1989) *Rich Law, Poor Law*, Buckingham: Open University Press.

Croall, H. (1993) 'White Collar Crime: 'Scams, Cons and Rips Offs'', *Sociology Review*, November 23–26.

Croall, H. (1998) *Crime and Society*, London: Longman.

De Haan, W. (1991) 'Abolitionism and Crime Control: A Contradiction in Terms' in K. Stenson and D. Cowell (eds.) *The Politics of Crime Control*, London: Sage.

Devlin, A. (1998) *Invisible Women*, Winchester: Waterside Press.

Dickson, B. (1989) *The Legal System in Northern Ireland*, Belfast: SLS Legal Publications.

Douglas, J. (1967) *The Social Meaning of Suicide*, Princetown: Princetown University Press.

Downes, D. and Rock, P. (1989) (3rd ed.) *Understanding Deviance*, Oxford: Oxford University Press.

Durkheim, E. (1895) 'The Normal and the Pathological', extract from 'The Rules of Sociological Methods' reprinted in J. Muncie, E. McLaughlin and M. Langan (1996) (eds.) *Criminological Perspectives*, London: Sage.

Durkheim, E. (1897) (reprinted 1970) *Suicide*, London: Routledge.

Eaton, M. (1986) *Justice for Women*, Buckingham: Open University Press.

Emlsey, C. (1996) 'The Origins and Development of the Police' in E. McLaughlin and J. Muncie (eds.) *Controlling Crime*, London: Sage.

Emsley, C. (1997) 'The History of Crime and Crime Control Institutions' in M. Maguire, R. Morgan and R. Reiner (eds.) (2nd ed.) *The Oxford Handbook of Criminology*, Oxford: Oxford University Press.

Farrington, D. (1997) 'Human Development and Criminal Careers', in M. Maguire, R. Morgan and R. Reiner (eds.) (2nd ed.) *The Oxford Handbook of Criminology*, Oxford: Oxford University Press.

Farrington, D. and Dowds, E. (1985) 'Disentangling Criminal Behaviour and Police Reaction' in D. Farrington and J. Gudd (eds.) *Reaction to Crime*, Chichester: John Wiley.

Foucault, M. (1977) *Discipline and Punish*, London: Allen Lane.

Gelsthorpe, L. (1996) 'Critical Decisions in the Criminal Courts' in E. McLaughlin and J. Muncie (eds.) *Controlling Crime*, London: Sage.

Gelsthorpe, L. (1997) 'Feminism and Criminology' in M. Maguire, R. Morgan and R. Reiner (eds.) (2nd ed.) *The Oxford Handbook of Criminology*, Oxford: Oxford University Press.

Gelsthorpe, L. and Morris, A. (1990) 'Introduction: Transforming and Transgressing Criminology' in L. Gelsthorpe and A. Morris (eds.) *Feminist Perspectives in Criminology*, Buckingham: Open University Press.

Gibbs, J. and Martin, W. (1964) *Status Integration and Suicide*, Oregon: University of Oregon Press.

Giddens, A. (1977) *Studies in Social and Political Theory*, London: Hutchinson.

Giddens, A. (1984) *The Constitution of Society*, Cambridge: Polity Press.

Gouldner, A. (1968) 'The Sociologist as Partisan: Sociology and the Welfare State', *American Sociologist*, 103–6.

Graham, P. and Clarke, J. (1996) 'Dangerous Places: Crime and the City' in J. Muncie and E. McLaughlin (eds.) *The Problem of Crime*, London: Sage.

Halbwachs, M. (1930) *Les Causes de Suicide*, Paris: Alcan.

Hall, R. (1985) *Ask Any Woman*, Bristol: Falling Wall Press.

Hall, S., Clarke, J., Critcher, C., Jefferson, T. and Roberts, B. (1978) *Policing the Crisis*, London: Macmillan.

Hanmer, J. and Saunders, S. (1984) *Well-Founded Fear*, London: Hutchinson.

Harding, R. (1997) *Private Prisons and Public Accountability*, Buckingham: Open University Press.

Hedderman, C. and Hough, M. (1994) *Does the Criminal Justice System Treat Men and Women Differently?*, Home Office Research Findings 10, London: HMSO.

Heidensohn, F. (1968) 'The Deviance of Women: A Critique and an Enquiry', *British Journal of Sociology*, 19: 160–75.

Heidensohn, F. (1989) *Crime and Society*, London: Macmillan.

Heidensohn, F. (1995) 'Overview of 25 years of Feminist Criminology', *Criminal Justice Matters*, 19: 4–5.

Heidensohn, F. (1996) (2nd ed.) *Women and Crime*, London: Macmillan.

Heidensohn, F. (1997) 'Gender and Crime', in M. Maguire, R. Morgan and R. Reiner (eds.) *The Oxford Handbook of Criminology*, Oxford: Oxford University Press.

Herek, G. and Berrill, K. (1992) *Hate Crimes*, Newbury Park, Ca.: Sage.

Home Office (1998) *Criminal Statistics for England and Wales 1997*, London: HMSO.

Hood, R. (1992) *Race and Sentencing*, Oxford: Clarendon Press.

Horn, R. (1995) 'Not Real Criminals: Police Perceptions of Women Offenders', *Criminal Justice Matters*, 19: 17–8.

Hough, M. and Mayhew, P. (1993) *The 1982 British Crime Survey*, London: HMSO.

Hulsman, L. (1986) 'Critical Criminology and the Concept of Crime', *Contemporary Crises*, 10: 63–80.

Ignatieff, M. (1978) *A Just Measure of Pain*, London: Macmillan.

Jefferson, T. (1997) 'Masculinities and Crimes' in M. Maguire, R. Morgan and R. Reiner (eds.) (2nd ed.) *The Oxford Handbook of Criminology*, Oxford: Oxford University Press.

Johnston, L. (1992) *The Rebirth of Private Policing*, London: Routledge.

Jones, M. (1998) 'Suicide Revisited', *Sociology Review*, September, 32–33.

Jones, T., Maclean, B. and Young, J. (1986) *The Islington Crime Survey*, Aldershot: Gower.

Jones, T., and Newburn, T. (1998) *Private Security and Public Policing*, Oxford: Oxford University Press.

Jupp, V. (1996) 'Contours of Criminology' in R. Sapsford (ed.) *Researching Crime and Criminal Justice*, Open University Course Material for D315.

Kituse, J. and Dietrick, D. (1959) 'Delinquent Boys: A Critique', *American Sociological Review*, 24: 208–15.

Klein, D. (1973) 'The Etiology of Female Crime: A Review of the Literature', *Issues in Sociology*, 8: 3–30.

Koffman, L. (1996) *Crime Surveys and Victims of Crime*, Cardiff: University of Wales Press.

Landau, S. and Nathan, G. (1983) 'Selecting Delinquents for Cautioning in the London Metropolitan Area', *British Journal of Criminology*, 23: 128–48.

Langan, M. (1996) 'Hidden and Respectable: Crime and the Market' in J. Muncie and E. McLaughlin (eds.) *The Problem of Crime*, London: Sage.

Lee, D. and Newby, H. (1983) *The Problem of Sociology*, London: Hutchinson.

Lees, S. (1986) *Losing Out*, London: Unwin.

Lees, S. (1993) *Sugar and Spice*, Harmondsworth: Penguin.

Lemert, E. (1951) *Social Pathology*, New York: McGraw-Hill.

Liazos, A. (1972) 'The Poverty of the Sociology of Deviance: Nuts, Sluts and Perverts', *Social Problems*, 20: 103–20.

Liberty (1992) *Unequal Before the Law*, London: Liberty.

Lombroso, C. (1876) *L'Uomo Delinquente*, Milan: Hoepli.

Lombroso, C. and Ferrero, W. (1895) *The Female Offender*, London: Fisher Unwin.

McLaughlin, E. (1996a) 'Political Violence, Terrorism and Crimes of the State' in J. Muncie and E. McLaughlin (eds.) *The Problem of Crime*, London: Sage.

McLaughlin, E. (1996b) 'Police, Policing and Policework' in E. McLaughlin and J. Muncie (eds.) *Controlling Crime*, London: Sage.

McLaughlin, E. and Muncie, J. (1998) 'The Sage Dictionary of Criminology', *British Society of Criminology Newsletter*, No. 31, p. 8.

Maguire, M. (1997) 'Crime Statistics, Patterns and Trends: Changing Perceptions and their Implication' in M. Maguire, R. Morgan and R. Reiner (eds.) (2nd ed.) *The Oxford Handbook of Criminology*, Oxford: Oxford University Press.

Mair, G. and Mortimer, E. (1996) *Curfew Orders with Electronic Monitoring*, London: HMSO.

Mair, G. and Nee, C. (1990) *Electric Monitoring: The Trials and their Results*, London: HMSO.

Matza, D. (1964) *Delinquency and Drift*, New York: Wiley.

Mayhew, P. and White, P. (1996) *The 1996 International Crime Victimisation Survey*, London: HMSO.

Mead, G. (1934) *Mind, Self and Society*, Chicago: University of Chicago Press.

Mednick, S., Moffit, T. and Stack, S. (1987) (eds.) *The Causes of Crime: New Biological Approaches*, Cambridge: Cambridge University Press.

Merton, R. (1938) 'Social Structure and Anomie', *American Sociological Review*, 3: 672–82.

Merton, R. (1957) *Social Theory and Social Structure*, New York: Free Press.

Miller, W. (1958) 'Lower Class Culture as a Generating Milieu of Gang Delinquency, *Journal of Social Issues*, 14: 5–19.

Mirrlees–Black, C., Mayhew, P. and Percy, A. (1996) *The 1996 British Crime Survey*, London: HMSO.

Mirrlees-Black, C., Budd, T., Partridge, S. and Mayhew, P. (1998) *The 1998 British Crime Survey*, London: HMSO.

Morris, A. (1987) *Women, Crime and Criminal Justice*, Oxford: Basil Blackwell.

Muncie, J. (1996) 'The Construction and Deconstruction of Crime' in J. Muncie and E. McLaughlin (eds.) *The Problem of Crime*, London: Sage.

Murray, C. (1990) *The Emerging Underclass*, London: IEA.

NACRO (1998) *Safer Society* (October), London: NACRO.

Newburn, T. and Stanko, E. (1994) (eds.) *Just Boys Doing Business*, London: Routledge.

Norris, C., Fielding, N., Kemp, C. and Fielding, J. (1992) 'Black and Blue: An Analysis of Race on Being Stopped by the Police', *British Journal of Sociology*, 43: 207–24.

Norris, C., Moran, J. and Armstong, G. (1998) *Surveillance, CCTV and Social Control*, Aldershot: Ashgate.

Park, R., Burgess, E. and McKenzie, R. (1925) *The City*, Chicago: University of Chicago Press.

Pearce, F. (1976) *Crimes of the Powerful*, London: Pluto.

Pease, K. (1997) 'Crime Prevention' in M. Maguire, R. Morgan and R. Reiner (eds.) (2nd ed.) *The Oxford Handbook of Criminology*, Oxford: Oxford University Press.

Pollak, O. (1961) *The Criminality of Women*, New York: A.S. Barnes.

Pope, W. (1976) *Durkheim's Suicide*, Chicago: University of Chicago Press.

Quinney, R. (1977) *Class, State and Crime*, Harlow: Longman.

Rock, P. (1994) 'The Social Organisation of British Criminology' in M. Maguire, R. Morgan and R. Reiner (eds.) (1st ed.) *The Oxford Handbook of Criminology*, Oxford: Oxford University Press.

Rock, P. (1996) *Reconstructing a Women's Prison*, Oxford: Clarendon Press.

Rozenberg, J. (1992) 'Miscarriages of Justice' in E. Stockdale and S. Casale (eds.) *Criminal Justice Under Stress*, London: Blackstone Press.

Saraga, E. (1996) 'Dangerous Places: The Family as a Site of Crime' in J. Muncie and E. McLaughlin (eds.) *The Problem of Crime*, London: Sage.

Schihor, D. (1995) *Punishment for Profit*, Thousand Oaks, Ca.: Sage.

Scraton, P. and Chadwick, K. (1991) 'The Theoretical and Political Priorities of Critical Criminology' in K. Stenson and D. Cowell (eds.) *The Politics of Crime Control*, London: Sage.

Sharpe, J. (1996) 'Crime, Order and Historical Change' in J. Muncie and E. McLaughlin (eds.) *The Problem of Crime*, London: Sage.

Shaw, C. (1930) *The Jack Roller: A Delinquent Boy's Own Story*, Chicago: University of Chicago Press.

Shaw, C. and McKay, H. (1942) *Juvenile Delinquency and Urban Areas*, Chicago: University of Chicago Press.

Shearing, C. and Stenning, P. (1985) 'From the Panopticon to Disney World: The Development of Discipline' in A. Doob and E. Greenspan (eds.) *Perspectives in Criminal Law*, Ontario: Canada Law Book Inc.

Simon, R. (1975) *Women and Crime*, London: Lexington Books.

Smart, C. (1976) *Women, Crime and Criminology*, London: Routledge.

Smart, C. (1990) 'Feminist Approaches to Criminology or Post-modern Woman Meets Atavistic Man' in L. Gelsthorpe and A. Morris (eds.) *Feminist Perspectives in Criminology*, Buckingham: Open University Press.

Smith, D. (1997) 'Ethnic Origins, Crime and Criminal Justice', in M. Maguire, R. Morgan and R. Reiner (eds.) (2nd ed.) *The Oxford Handbook of Criminology*, Oxford: Oxford University Press.

Smith, D. and Gray, J. (1985) *Police and the Public in London*, Aldershot: Gower.

Social Trends (1997) London, HMSO.

Stanko, E. (1990) 'When Precaution is Normal: A Feminist Critique of Crime Prevention' in L. Gelsthorpe and A. Morris (eds.) *Feminist Perspectives in Criminology*, Buckingham: Open University Press.

Sutherland, E. (1947) *Principles of Criminology*, Philadelphia: Lippincott.

Sutherland, E. (1949) *White-Collar Crime*, New York: Holt, Reinhart and Winston.

Sykes, G. and Matza, D. (1957) 'Techniques of Neutralization', *American Sociological Review*, 22: 664–673.

Taylor, I., Walton, P. and Young, J. (1973) *The New Criminology*, London: Routledge.

Taylor, S. (1988) *Suicide*, London: Longman.

Thrasher, F. (1927) *The Gang*, Chicago: University of Chicago Press.

Tischler, H. (1996) (5th ed.) *Introduction to Sociology*, Orlando: Harcourt Brace College Publishers.

Tong, R. (1998) (2nd ed.) *Feminist Thought*, London: Routledge.

Walklate, S. (1996) 'Community and Crime Prevention' in E. McLaughlin and J. Muncie (eds.) *Controlling Crime*, London: Sage.

Walmsley, R. Howard, L. and White, S. (1992) *The National Prison Survey 1991: Main Findings*, Home Office Research Study 128, London: HMSO.

Whyte, W. (1943) *Street Corner Society*, Chicago: University of Chicago Press.

Wikstrom, P. (1991) *Urban Crime, Criminals and Victims*, New York: Springer-Verlag.

Wilson, J. (1975) *Thinking About Crime*, New York: Vintage.

Wilkins, L. (1964) *Social Deviance*, London: Tavistock.

Yablonsky, L. (1962) *The Violent Gang*, London: Paladin.

Young, J. (1986) 'The Failure of Criminology: The Need for Radical Realism' in R. Matthews and J. Young (eds.) *Confronting Crime*, London: Sage.

Young, J. (1994) 'Incessant Chatter: Recent Paradigms in Criminology' in M. Maguire, R. Morgan and R. Reiner (eds.) (1st ed.) *The Oxford Handbook of Criminology*, Oxford: Oxford University Press.

Young, J. (1997) 'Left Realist Criminology: Radical in its Analysis, Realist in its Policy' in M. Maguire, R. Morgan and R. Reiner (eds.) (2nd ed.) *The Oxford Handbook of Criminology*, Oxford: Oxford University Press.

Young, J. and Matthew, R. (1992) (eds.) *Rethinking Criminology*, London: Sage.

Young, P. and Young, M. (1994) *Crime and Criminal Justice in Scotland*, Edinburgh: The Scottish Office.

Zedner, L. (1997) 'Victims' in M. Maguire, R. Morgan and R. Reiner (eds.) *The Oxford Handbook of Criminology*, Oxford: Oxford University Press.

INDEX